101 TIPS AND HINTS FOR YOUR BOAT

101 TIPS AND HINTS FOR YOUR BOAT

by
Jacques Damour

Translated by Jeremy Howard-Williams

W W Norton & Company
New York and London

© Granada Publishing 1981

First American edition 1981

All rights reserved

Printed in Great Britain

ISBN 0-393-03262-0

Contents

Dangers offshore are certainly very real but, strange as it may seem, accidents occur more often on the moorings, coming alongside or in port generally. The average boat is often better equipped to put to sea than she is to remain in dock. As far as keelboats are concerned, instruction is far more often about handling the boat in open waters, than moving about among moorings, buoys and the busy waterways of a port.

A lot of unnecessary time is spent on many boats in pulling wrong sails from bags, fighting them on deck, and then struggling to control them when they are up. Anything which can help reduce this effort must be useful.

What they call 'safety equipment', that which is required under the rules, seems to me to be badly named. It is much more last ditch equipment, which should never have to be used except for practice. Safety consists of other matters, and is more a state of mind. It means having certain skills, great attention to detail, not a little imagination, combined with what my father used to call a good guardian angel to keep you from indiscretion and stop you from taking silly risks — it's not fear, but a sense of responsibility and an appreciation of the odds.

Preface

The links which tie a man to a boat are many and varied. For those who look on her as a method of relaxation and escape, she is merely a means to an end. Others, of whom I am one, cherish her as a living thing.

The first kind of skipper spends his winters dreaming of the opening cruise of next spring; he is quite happy to hire a boat — any boat so long as it will do the job. The others think as much, or even more, about the boat as about the sailing; this kind nearly always becomes an owner sooner or later.

The escapists tell tales of their passage making, of fishing trips, of the gales they have survived. The rest of us have the same tall tales, of course, but the conversation always eventually returns to the same subject — the boat herself. We talk endlessly of useful gadgets we have seen on other boats, of tricks whereby some chore can be made easier or some drill made less irksome.

And basically that's what we like best: to turn what starts off as just any boat into something special, an expression of our own personality.

I'm sure that by not weighing anchor at various times and for various reasons — real or imaginary — I have missed some good sailing. But by staying in harbour I have also been able to poke around other boats spotting ideas, picking the brains of other owners, so that what may have started off as one of a hundred identical production line craft has been given individuality and character, through clever gadgets and bright ideas built in over the years. More than once such inquisitiveness has ended by exchanging notes with other proud inventors, accompanied as a rule by the popping of corks.

And so I felt it worth while to present a selection of those tips, hints, improvements or stratagems, call them what you like, which I have spotted and copied on various cruises all over the world. Many of them have been developed for a specific need by experienced sailors, but can still be just the thing for the average cruising man or woman. Each one reminds me just where and how I first saw it . . .

I Deckwork

Temporary Mooring

When the wind is pushing you off, arrival at a quay or alongside another boat can be interesting — especially with a reduced crew.

To make sure that you are not going to be blown away, you must get a temporary line on board, so that the main springs and breast lines can then be made fast at leisure.

There is not usually any fairlead specially provided for this sort of temporary attachment, so you may have to look to your genoa track or perforated toe-rail for some sort of makeshift lead. It should be led just forward of amidships.

A single whip, consisting of a length of line with a plastic covered S hook at one end and rove through a turning block fixed to your deck with a snap shackle, will be ideal for hooking onto the base of a stanchion. Easy to haul taut, either by hand or on the winch, it will hold you steady until the proper mooring lines can be made up. Be careful to hook the base and not the top of the stanchion, and don't do it if your boat has too much way on.

Extra Cleats on a Sandwich Core Deck

Sandwich construction makes it difficult to add stressed fittings at points not previously strengthened to take them, through the replacement of the lightweight balsa or foam filling by solid wood which can accept bolts and spread the load efficiently.

There is absolutely no need to throw your hands in the air and give in, because backing pads, glued to the outer laminate (which must be properly cleaned and prepared) can ensure firm fixing.

For a mooring cleat, the plywood pad on the deck should be ¾in thick and twice the length of the cleat x one length broad. Under the deck, if big washers are fitted to the bolts to help spread the load, the thickness of the pad can be reduced a bit, but not less than ⅜in.

Don't forget to use a mastic filler between the various layers to make sure that the result will be watertight.

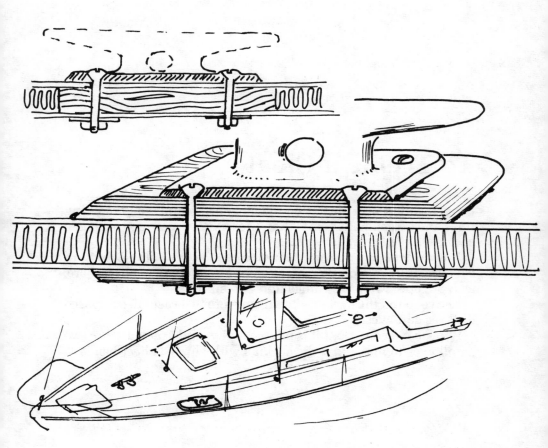

To Treble a Cleat

Overcrowding at a port often means more complicated mooring lines and attachment points than those with which modern boats seem to have been equipped.

It is difficult to make up, adjust or cast off on a single forward cleat the full hand of five lines which can sometimes collect there: a head rope, two breast lines and two springs.

I have found the system shown opposite to be useful, composed of three soft eyes.

Slipped over the cleat it is not too bulky, and I then use the two small eyes to make fast the springs with slipped sheet bends.

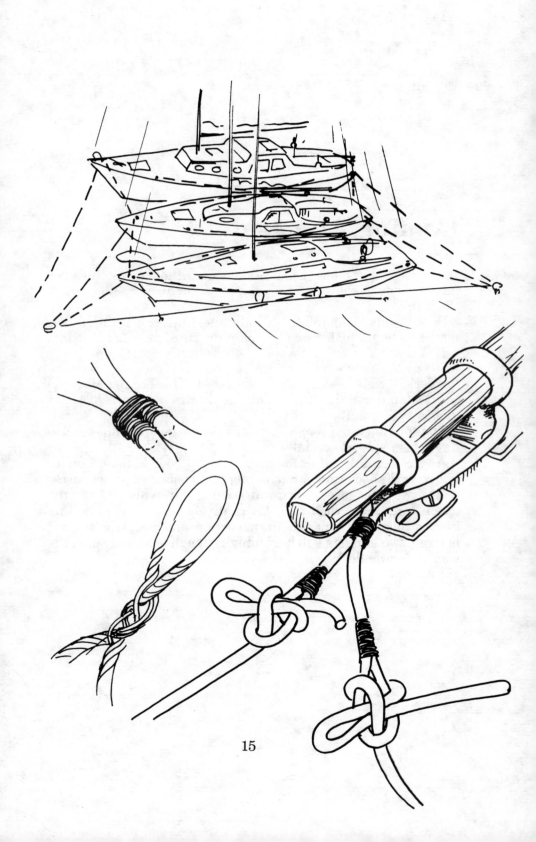

Coming Alongside

It is seldom that a boat comes alongside without a crew member having to dash below, at the last minute, for an extra line to help the final moor up.

Small boats using relatively light lines, and even some of their bigger sisters, finish by collecting a tangle of assorted knitting.

No matter how well they are coiled, a short length is practically never available when it is needed, especially if that need is on the foredeck — right now. Sod's Law (or that of his brother Murphy) sees to it that there is always someone sitting on the vital locker at moments like that.

The solution is to prepare one or two spare mooring lines and to have them stowed specially.

Any coiled halyard or mooring line can be held neatly under two rows of shock cord, stretched across a coachroof or clear deck. Space two rows of eye straps at six inch intervals and run the shock cord under each row. Alternatively a shock cord sail tie hooked round the upper lifeline makes a useful hanger. If the coil is large, two hangers will hold it high enough to keep it out of the way of feet on deck.

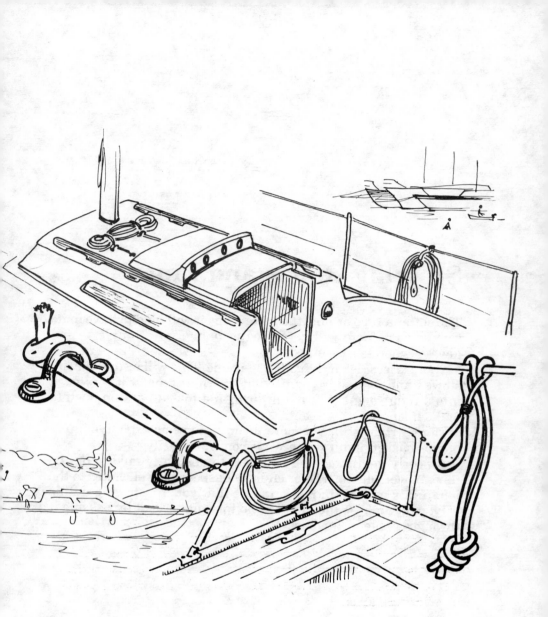

Stowing Ropes and Lines

The softer a rope or line, the more loops it will tend to have in its coil, so that there will be a greater danger of a tangle — and always when least wanted.

There is less risk if the coil is a big one. This will be more easily stowed and, indeed, recognised at the right time, if it is twisted into a figure eight with a half turn, and folded back on itself to make it smaller.

More certain still, but more inconvenient, pay the line into a bag or basket and it will always come out easily.

A poorly ventilated bag can lead to unsightly mildew on the rope. Woven plastic fruit or laundry baskets are well suited to the job. If it is your main mooring line that you are stowing in this way, you can keep the tail to hand for making fast by passing it through a hole in the basket.

There are Moorings and Moorings

You can drop anchor for half an hour's swim, for lunch or for a nap; on the other hand, if you decide to go ashore, the boat will be left unattended for several hours.

If your type of sailing involves frequent stops and you are, perhaps, on the lazy side, you could be forgiven for wondering if the somewhat prudent motto 'better be safe than sorry' doesn't involve rather too much work for the crew.

On the other hand it's worth remembering that all anchors don't hold equally well on all bottoms.

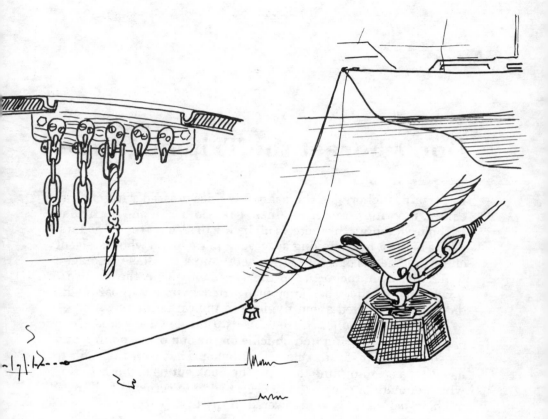

To be sure of a system suitable for every circumstance, I have sorted out my ground tackle. I now have a rack on which is hung the throat or anchor end of each rode, complete with its shackle.

There are two lengths of chain ready, one of 15 feet and one of 30 feet, and they can either be used individually or together, between the anchor and the rope rode. A rope rode is often best on a rocky bottom, but you may not always use it if it is not immediately to hand. Finally, there is something to weigh down the line.

I have a Danforth anchor, which holds well in weed, and a CQR which stays in the bow fairlead.

Don't Forget the Tripping Line

In certain anchorages the seabed is criss-crossed with chains, cables, moorings and cross lines. I remember in one particular harbour watching three crews all trying to recover their anchors.

The biggest boat, having succeeded in raising a whole stack of chains by means of a roped grapnel round a windlass, managed to free her own anchor when the whole lot was at the surface.

One of the others had a stout hearted swimmer aboard, who didn't seem worried about hygiene in the rather dirty water.

The third boat pulled her rode hard up and down, lowered a loop of chain over the ring and shackle on the end of the shank, and eased it up against the arms of the anchor. They were then able to use it as a tripping line to heave the hook out backwards (a line which should, of course, have been tied to the crown of all three anchors before they were lowered in the first place).

There are Anchors and Anchors

If you anchor frequently, as when coastal cruising, it can become tiring to have to lift the hook over the pulpit every time.

A CQR is best stowed with its stock right in the bow fairlead and the rode pulled tight, so that the pivot point of the fluke is hard against the roller — always supposing that the forestay isn't in the way.

A Danforth can be conveniently mounted by two rings on one of the pulpit uprights, looped over the stock. Any other balanced fluke or bar anchor can be stowed in the stern pulpit.

An anchor and rode are best kept from snarling in the locker by being stowed in a canvas pocket or even an old sailbag. This makes it more sure that the line will run cleanly when required.

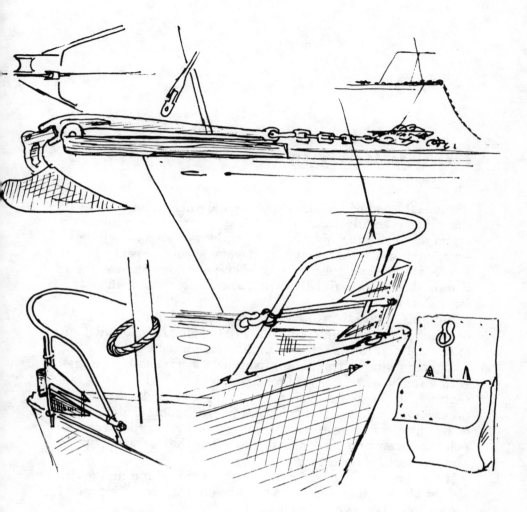

Rocky Bottom

Right at the end of a Mediterranean cape where I sometimes sail there is a small isolated anchorage, which is perfect for swimming or sunbathing in fine weather, or for snorkelling or scuba diving. There is even a fresh water spring, sweet and clear where it wells out of the rock and, after it has flowed across one or two shallow pools to finish in a miniature waterfall, ideally warm for a shower.

But alas, such idylls often end by someone having to dive for the anchor, even though it may have a tripping line, to pull it out of the welter of rocks into which it hooks all too easily.

Lighter than the traditional fisherman's stone, a big grapnel with a fairly 'soft' hook will hold well on a rocky bottom in fine weather; it can be recovered by pulling the hooks straight if necessary. If it gets completely jammed by the shank, not a great deal will be lost because these grapnels aren't very expensive. The point to remember is to double up the line so that it can be slipped and recovered if necessary.

If you are at a biggish port, some galvanised rod and a vice should allow you to renew the lost hook at little cost. Opposite I have shown two ways of doing this.

Gaff!

'All hands fend off!'

Shouts, cries, tumult. Failure to pick up the mooring buoy first go can have nasty consequences: crushed fingers and bent pulpits are frequently the result.

The small mooring buoy rarely has an eye large enough to be easily grabbed and, if you have your own permanent mooring, it is a good idea to guard against this problem. A short length of floating line with a baby float on the end will make things a lot simpler.

Rather than hang onto a mooring float with a gaff until one of the crew can pass a line through it, a temporary attachment can be hooked on by means of a 'Grabit' boathook. This carries a line attached to a kind of extra large carbine hook, fixed to the end of the gaff by shock cord or some other quick release. When the hook snaps onto the float ring, the line is pulled clear of the gaff, leaving a direct link with the mooring.

Portable Clam Cleats

On most small boats, only the main mooring cable will have a diameter large enough for a crewman to get a real pull on it. Tackles and modern winches allow the others to be of a more modest size, quite big enough for the forces involved.

For reasons of economy, mooring lines and spare warps will usually be the same diameter as the sheets (they will, indeed, often be old sheets). Thus, if the main mooring cable is too short for the berth chosen, it will be necessary to join on a length of thinner line.

If it blows up, this can make getting under way a rather painful process; if the anchor is solidly stuck in blue clay, the thin line can be murder on the hands.

The docker's hook inspired the tip in the upper part of my picture. A side-fixed clam cleat bolted to a hand grip enables full force to be exerted on a small diameter rope, which would otherwise cut the hands.

Another twist to the same theme: a strap and eye added to the grip will enable the load to be taken on a jib sheet which has a riding turn on the winch; or else, by only losing an inch or two, to transfer the weight of a sheet to a cleat, thus freeing the winch for another purpose.

Bad Weather Tiller Extension

The small aft cockpit which separates the helmsman from too close a contact with the winch gorillas has, like the wheel, its firm protagonists. But even in a conventional cockpit you can get isolated, and the tiller extension inherited from the dinghy boys now comes into its own. It enables the helmsman to get right up to the forward end of the cockpit under the protection of the main bulkhead, where he can see what's going on, and still steer properly.

Thus, when you are close hauled in the cold of a windy dawn, you may be less *à la mode*, but you can snuggle up against the cabin bulkhead protected from wind and spray (even if there's no dodger).

A tiller extension is easily made of metal tube, or wood with a metal sleeve. As I have indicated, it is most appreciated in the early morning, but it can also be useful if the helm becomes difficult in strong winds, because it gives added leverage.

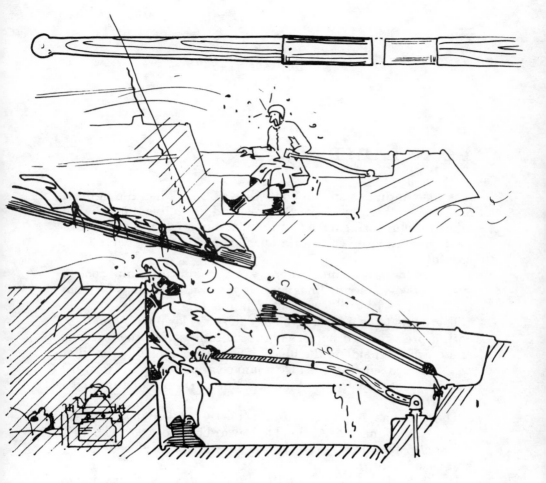

Yoke Lines

It is fascinating to steer a boat when racing, when the lightest pressure on the tiller makes her respond like a live thing; but to take the helm during a long stint under motor in a flat calm, with the sun beating down from a burnished sky, can be more than painful.

The foredeck is so much more restful, comfortable and cool. A system of yoke steering lines enables you to stretch out as far from the engine as possible, without relinquishing control.

There has to be a turning block each side, level with the tiller, with a pre-stretched polyester line running across the foredeck and down each side to the block, whence it can lead to the tiller end. On each side there is also a jam cleat placed at the forward end of the coachroof, so that the yoke line can be blocked against a pull aft.

The tiller has the windward yoke line rigged, leaving the one to leeward disconnected; it is held to leeward by shock cord. There is thus only one control to work: it is pulled in order to bear away, and eased to luff.

It is a good idea to back up the shock cord with a check line to limit its stretch. In this way a fierce yaw won't allow the boat to bear away too far.

This kind of system is also well suited to solo navigators, or those who are the only ones aboard who can sail. I was once able to hand over to a real landlubber without any more instructions than to push, pull or middle it. In spite of these simple directions, we had a critical moment when my non-sailing yokeman decided to change tacks 'just to see what would happen.'

II   Sail handling

Headsails

Racing boats striving for the smallest part of a knot in their unending search for speed have had a whole stack of new headsails developed for them: tallboy, blooper, big boy, tri-radial etc., all of them not only photogenic, but highly efficient when they are set and trimmed by hard racing crews working all round the clock.

The performance of these specialist sails is not so attractive to cruising yachtsmen that they are prepared to give them locker space against the few occasions when they are likely to use them. There is thus no question of considering these exotic items in this book, which is more concerned with simplifying the mundane tasks which the open sea always demands.

However, many cruises take place in boats which are racing machines. Such craft have large fore-triangles, which the racing rule has favoured of late, and these require a lot of crew forward of the mast for sail handling. So we shall discuss headsail handling in general and also the spinnaker which, in spite of all the gear it needs, is now known to respond to a little kindness (I know it can look beautiful too), especially in fine weather.

Quickly dealt with by strong, well trained crews, these sails are not so easy for cruising craft. But should you find yourself aboard a hot-rod with the family, the following tips might help to make life easier.

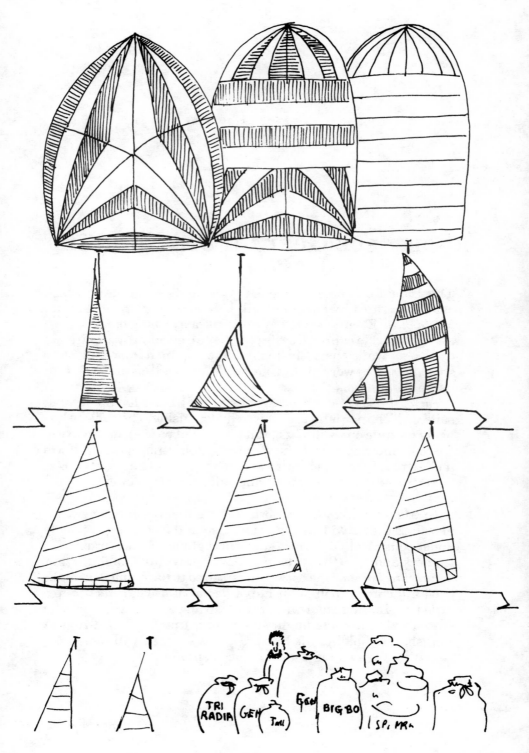

Foredeck Gear for Jib Handling

'One hand for yourself and one for the boat', so anything which can be operated by one hand will be welcome on the foredeck.

Shackles. Even if secured by a seizing or a locking pin, and even if a key shackle cannot lose its pin, they all eventually require two hands to work them. Piston plunger snap hanks and snap shackles can be worked with one hand, and are thus preferable for halyards and tack fittings.

Tack Strops. Decksweeping jibs are all right for racing, but sails with shorter luffs are preferred for cruising. They will be less likely to chafe on the lifeline, run less risk of picking up a wave in the foot, and won't block the view of the helmsman so much. Twin tack strops, each fitted with a snap shackle, will allow two jibs to be rigged at the same time during sail changes — or even all the time.

To Muzzle a Jib. Some sort of permanent arrangement for muzzling the jib will be appreciated, so that it can be got quickly under control while the new sail is brought up. Shock cord across the deck and up to the top pulpit rail will prove invaluable for this.

Halyard Points. One or two rings, seized to the pulpit, will make good attachment points for halyards out of use or attached to a furled jib. Having before now nearly swung ashore while holding onto a halyard made up on shock cord, I prefer a solid ring. A ring shackle holding the halyard to the forestay will sometimes stop it flying away if it is let go accidentally.

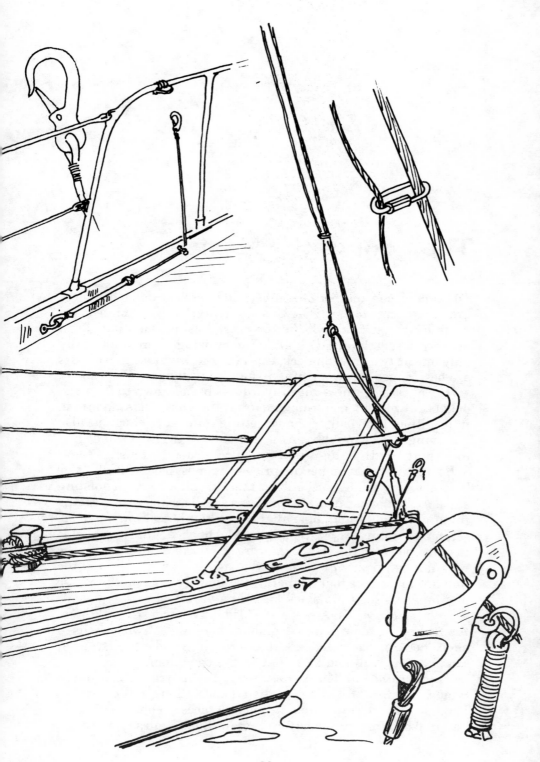

The Foot of the Mast

To bring all controls back to the cockpit is all very well when there are enough crewmen to work them properly. But if one man has to do it by himself, he will be for ever chasing back and forth between foredeck and cockpit. When cruising, there are usually only one or two crew on deck, especially at night, so most boats are best rigged for everything to happen at the foot of the mast.

Halyards. The tail of the halyard has been known to fly away out of control, which is annoying to say the least; if it is made fast, it is difficult to coil without getting tangled, which is also annoying. These problems can be avoided if the tail is made fast to a short length of light line which can take the twist.

Hoisting. Mast winches are pricey and most people think twice before buying them, especially as there are other ways of hoisting sails. A cleat on a track, attached to a small tackle, will allow the final inches to be got home after the halyard has been made up.

Simpler than that, a small tackle hooked onto a shackle inserted between the end of the wire halyard and the start of the rope tail can be used to take in the last tension. Hand haul the halyard and make fast temporarily, then sweat up on the tackle and make up the final slack on the halyard.

Stowing Halyards. A mass of coiled halyards festooned round the foot of the mast is messy and unseamanlike. Two lengths of shock cord, spaced a foot apart and running under eye straps at 6in stations, will hold them flat on the coachroof.

Winch Handles. The seabed must be littered with dropped winch handles! To increase their expectation of life, fix two lengths of shock cord round the mast. A piece of split plastic hose will make it easier to insert and retain the handles.

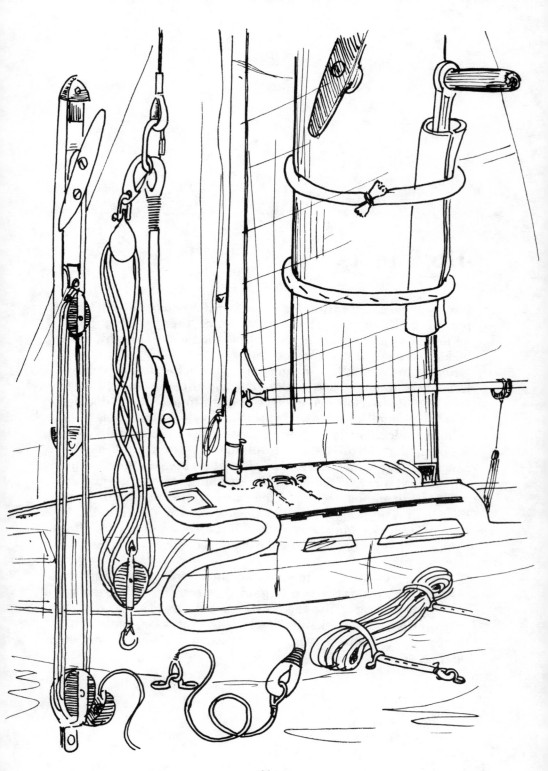

41

Jib Sheets

I know of no metal fitting for attaching sheets to a jib which has proved infallible; they have all at some time or other flown undone, refused to open at the critical moment, or else hit some luckless crewman hard on the head.

Some kind of textile attachment is much better: less expensive, less likely to seize, less bulky. The top illustration is a good example, if the clew eye is large enough to accept the doubled sheet. The small strop seized to the sheet eye locks the whole thing solidly, undoes easily and never comes adrift accidentally.

The modern jib often has a triangular clew or a stainless steel ring or D-ring, which are all easier to fit securely to the clew, but which need a rather more complicated sheet arrangement.

The strop and ball seized to the sheets is effective (centre) and easy to fit. The stopper can take the form of a simple figure eight knot or a bulkier Matthew Walker. If it's elegance you are after, then a monkey's fist on the end of a spliced line is all the rage, so they tell me.

If a decksweeping jib means that the clew is almost into the fairlead, an inch or two can be gained by seizing the two ends of the stopper direct to the sheet with waxed thread.

Use of a racking seizing, in which the turns are put on in a figure of eight, will prevent the two parts of the strop moving against each other.

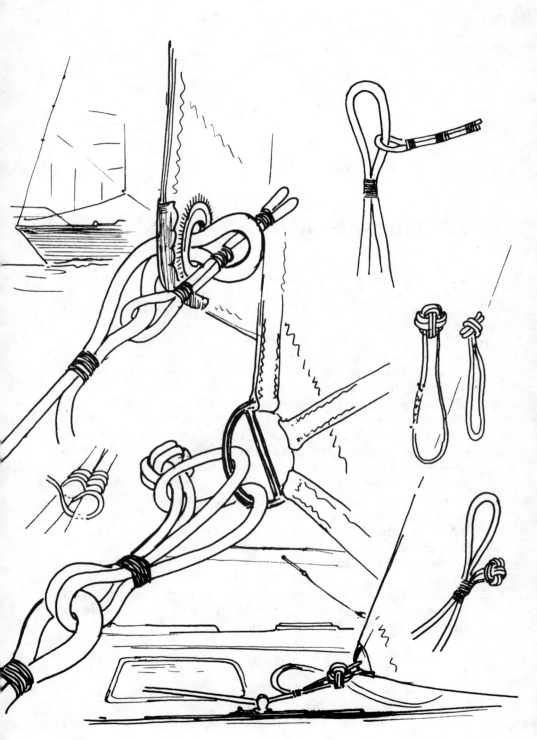

43

Jib Downhaul

In racing, speed in jib changing is vital in order not to leave the boat bald headed for too long. If three crewmen are necessary, they'll fall over each other — which is all supposed to be part of the fun.

It's not quite the same when cruising. The crew are fewer, they are not so experienced, nor do they have the pressure. Thus anything which can cut down the need for bodies on the foredeck must be right.

A downhaul permanently attached to the jib halyard is useful. It immediately replaces one man on the foredeck, because it enables a man at the mast to bring the jib head down to the deck and to hold it there until the sail is muzzled (you will no doubt have noticed how a jib can refuse to come down below half way, preferring to flog at mid-hoist, especially if the boat is heeled to a fresh breeze). It also ensures that the halyard doesn't fly away out of control by mistake.

A turning block at the bottom of the forestay will let it run to a fairlead, whence it can pass to a cleat by the mast or on the coachroof, near a canvas pocket where it can be conveniently stowed.

A small line of some ¼in diameter or ¾in circumference will be quite enough for boats up to 30ft LOA. It should run up inside the jib's piston hanks to stop it flogging.

Foredeck Jib Stowage

Fashion, stemming from the offshore scene, has given to the cruising man a big fore-triangle, which carries with it a requirement to switch headsails constantly if maximum speed is to be obtained.

The smaller the boat, the more frequently must these tricky headsail changes take place. This in turn means that there is less room for the crew because the sails overflow their lockers.

To make sail changes easier, the working genoa and the No 1 jib should remain on the foredeck, permanently hanked to the stay.

When they are stowed on deck — genoa one side and working jib the other — the snap hanks are taken off the stay and clipped to a wire strop running the pulpit to a pad eye on deck. Nets can be rigged on the lifelines so that the sails can be easily stowed. Alternatively, short lengths of shock cord with eye and toggle can be fastened to stanchion bases to hold the sails tightly under control.

If the sails are stowed along the lifelines either in netting or shock cord, be careful that they do not mask the navigation lights or block the helmsman's view.

Jib Reefs

The business of constantly switching headsails on a small boat, in order to suit the weather, is a nuisance. Apart from the work involved on deck, it means bundling wet sails down into what is laughingly called the forward cabin.

A working genoa which can be reefed to an intermediate, and a No 1 which can become a No 2 make life a lot easier. Even if it means going forward to change the tack fixture, changing the sheets to a new clew, and tying in a couple of reef points, the foredeck hand will be exposed to the elements for a shorter time than if he has to change sails.

If all controls come back to the cockpit and if there is a second set of sheets, most of the work can be done from aft.

Bend the new sheet up to the upper clew, ease the working sheet and the halyard slightly, take up on the wire downhaul, if one is fitted, to bring the new tack down to the deck, and then harden the halyard again. Trim the sheet and it's practically done.

A short time sailing dead before the wind will allow a dash onto the foredeck to tie in a couple of reef points under the lee of the mainsail. This will tidy up the slack sail near the clew; the part near the tack will be controlled by the lifeline.

Mainsails

Headsails give more drive for area than mainsails, provided they are properly set and trimmed. Racing rules, which usually measure the fore-triangle and not the sail area which it supports, have encouraged this emphasis on jibs — in spite of the fact that one or two recent designs have shown that it is possible to rate very well without a fore-triangle at all.

The cruising man would do well to resist these two extremes if possible. Personally, I prefer a reasonably sized mainsail; apart from anything else, its control is relatively easy and, if the system is properly thought out, reefing doesn't need anyone forward of the mast.

A fair-sized mainsail will also pull sufficiently well on a broad reach to make hoisting a spinnaker an unnecessary luxury.

Finally, except in certain hot-rods which may be unbalanced without a headsail, the mainsail is the best sail for easy boat handling in the confined waters of a crowded harbour if the engine has failed. It is thus worth considering carefully anything which makes its control simpler.

Slug Slides

For reasons of economy and, perhaps, ease of use, small cruising boats often have a mainsail which runs in a mast groove.

As soon as there is enough wind to prevent the sail from lying quietly, two are needed to hoist or lower it — one to work the halyard and one to feed the luff into the mast, or one to lower and one to stop the sail falling into the water.

It does not cost much to fit eyelets to the luff so that slug slides may be fitted to run in the mast groove, and they make control so much easier. Don't forget to have a stop to prevent them coming out at the bottom of the groove — either by a pin through the groove

or else a strop round the mast, held by a tang just higher than the groove entry.

The headboard needs special treatment. When reefed with the sheet hard in, the leech tends to pull the head away from the mast quite hard, and the halyard doesn't hold it in at all. Two slides (or one double) are advisable on the headboard because of this. A third, on the halyard eye itself, will not only help but will also stop any tendency for the halyard to fly away out of control when it is undone.

Slide attachment is easy. Two parts of cord should just go through the conical opening in the slug, and are then doubled on themselves and sewn down (more secure than seizing); the two doubled ends then jam perfectly.

Pulling down the Reef Pennant

If reefing in a hurry, there should be no need to go to the boom end to tie down the new clew — the reefing pennant should do it perfectly.

If the sail is flogging, it will need quite a lot of force to pull it down. Rather than a winch on the boom (with the danger that the handle can be lost), a small tackle can be rigged to pull a clam cleat along a track on the side of the boom.

Get in as much as possible on the reef pennant by hand, make fast on a horn cleat and then slip the pennant into the clam cleat. Harden the tackle and make up the slack on the horn cleat.

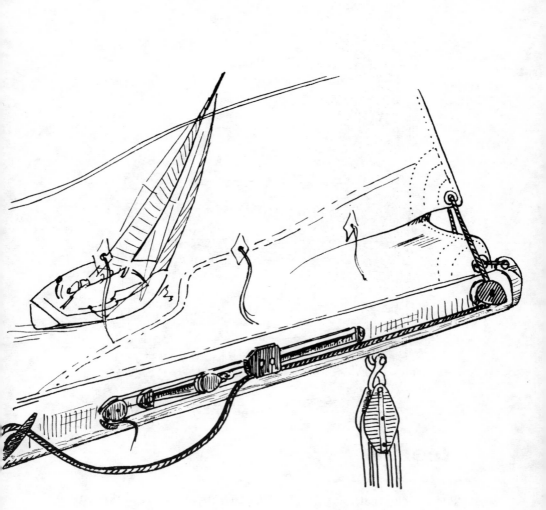

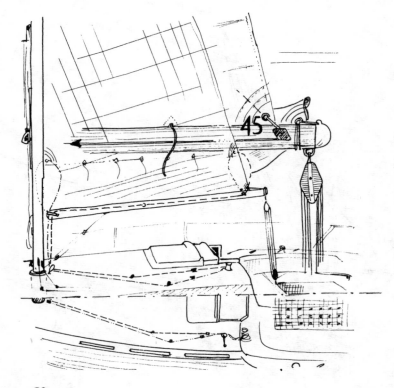

Reefing

The classic method of reefing by means of individual points on the sail is more secure, gives a better shaped sail and allows the boom vang to continue to work normally; it also has the advantage that it can be done almost entirely from the cockpit, apart from a quick dash on deck to make fast the new tack eye and one or two reef points.

But with only one fixed turning block for the reefing pennant, the shape has got to be right first time. Hence the importance of having the turning blocks (also called bee blocks or reef blocks) properly sited and a pennant which will not stretch.

It is also necessary to have some system of sweating hard on the pennant to make it really taut. There should, in fact, be five turning points in the clew reefing system, including the new clew

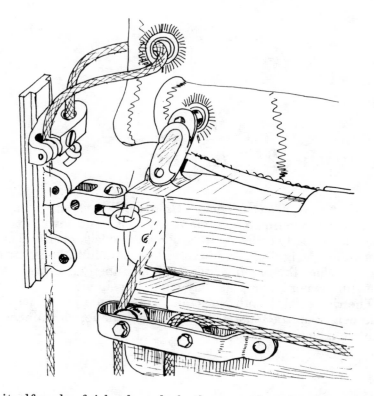

eye itself and a fairlead on deck; there are four for the tack reef pennant.

Clew Reef Pennant. The lead of the pennant, once the new clew has been pulled down, should make an angle of 45° with the boom (rising to 50° when the sail fills).

Tack Reef Pennant. If the gooseneck is fixed, the fairlead can be on the mast. It should lie at an angle of about 30° to the normal tack eye of the mainsail when set without a reef. If there is a sliding gooseneck, the lead can either be mounted on the slide or else on the boom itself.

Reef Eyelets. Remember that a reef taken by remotely operated pennants will pull the eyelets down to the boom less than one sweated in by hand and proper tensioning tackles. Reef points should thus either be tied more loosely, or else the tack and clew reef earrings should be fitted slightly higher than the line of reef points, which may then be tied in normally.

57

'Lazyjack' Furling

The old timers, even the ancient Chinese, discovered an easy way
to control the mainsail automatically as it came down, so that it
could be properly furled or, indeed, reefed, at leisure later. The one
or two extra rigging lines involved — quite light ones, for they
don't replace the topping lift — will be happily accepted by the
cruising owner as long as they make life simpler.

The rig is fitted both sides, and runs from a point just above
mid-height on the mast. Control is from the forward line which
runs to a cleat on the boom.

Spinnakers

Contrary to what you might suppose, it isn't essential to have a strong and aggressive crew to fly a kite. If the gear is carefully arranged, it can even be quite a pleasant sail.

The trick is to restrict the brute's appearance to fine weather with the wind well aft. Don't hesitate to take it down if the wind gets up and the crew is inexperienced.

The tips which follow are the result of many years experience, often on the race course. They will simplify control of a sail which can be useful as well as beautiful.

It is no longer essential to bag the spinnaker in a turtle, which requires room and some care, if it is kept in a sheath or a series of rings (Spee Squeezer or Spinnaker Sally). No more problems in lowering, if it is furled beforehand. No more crushed hands or mainsails damaged by crash gybing if the spinnaker pole always remains fixed in its mast cup.

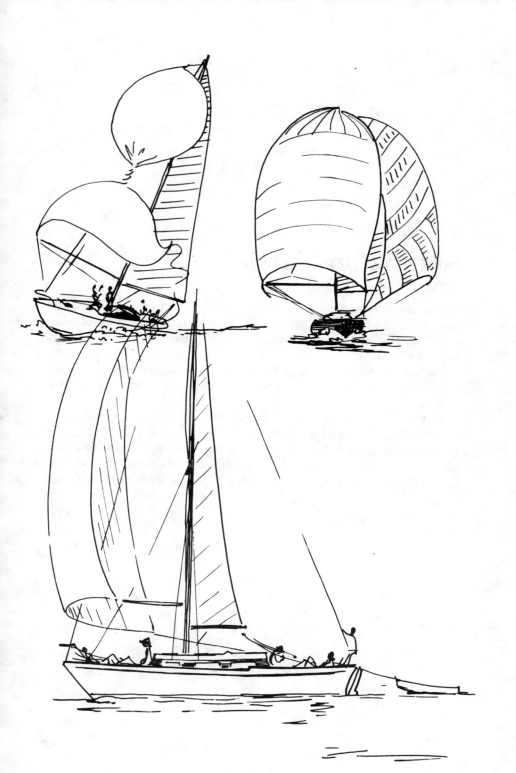

Spinnaker Turtle

If you don't have a Spee Squeezer or Sally — of which more later — it is usual to hoist the spinnaker from its bag, where it has been carefully packed. The bag is placed on the foredeck to leeward and near the bow.

Bags don't always remain properly closed while they wait, and they have been known to blow overboard if they aren't properly tied down.

Any sailbag can do the job, even if it hasn't got a lashing sewn to the bottom. A stone or a ball placed in the bottom of the bag will enable a line to be tied securely to it, so that it can be made fast to a cleat. Gather the bag round the stone and take a couple of turns round the neck of the pocket so formed. Pass one of the ends under the second round turn and then tie the two together. This will not easily come undone.

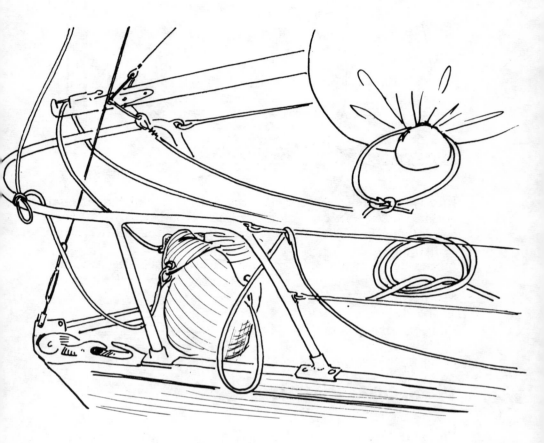

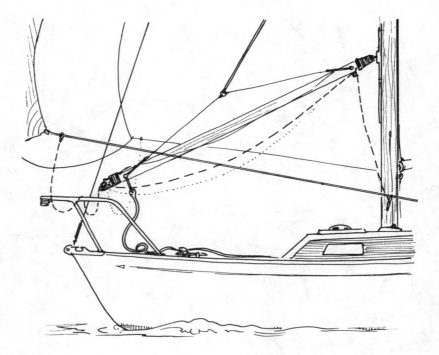

Easier Gybing

The standard procedure for gybing with a double ended pole entails four operations.

1. Take the pole off the mast.
2. Fit the old clew (or the sheet) into the newly freed pole end.
3. Release the new sheet.
4. Fit the pole back on the mast.

If the wind is at all fresh or if there is a swell so that the boat is rolling, this may be easier said than done.

The pole may not be prepared to submit docilely to steps 1 and 4 (it can show considerable resistance and strength, so watch out for your fingers!). Among other things, the clew seems to take a malicious pleasure in not wanting to be caught.

In the absence of an inner forestay, the dip-pole method is much easier.

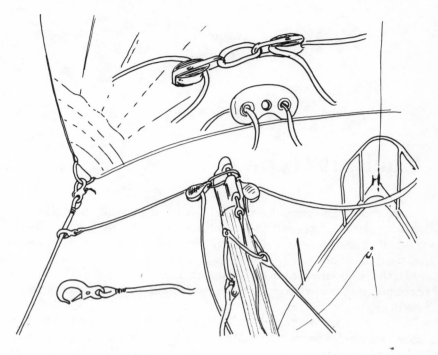

The spinnaker pole is connected to the two sheets by a line controlled from the mast. A strop with two blocks attached to the outer end of the pole will be necessary on boats over about 30 ft LOA — for smaller craft, the kind of 'kidney' shown above will do, provided the holes are well rounded off.

The drill is then as follows. Run off before the wind and equalise the guy and sheet. Raise the inboard end of the pole and ease the topping lift just enough to allow the pole to swing through the foretriangle without catching on the forestay or the pulpit (put a check mark on the lift slide). Ease the control line of the old tack/guy, haul in the other to draw the new guy down to the pole and make it fast, raise the topping lift. All contact with sharp items of equipment is avoided.

The only drawback is that the clew has rather too much weight in light weather. But that is the least of your worries when cruising.

Cockpit Gybe

There are spinnaker poles which have been specially designed for this operation. One end fits into the mast cup, and it has a cleat. The other end is rigged with two lines which run down the middle of the pole itself.

If the two lines and the topping lift are taken back to the cockpit, this allows a gybe to be controlled without having to go on deck.

This will be welcomed by those crew members who find the foredeck particularly unexciting, because it means that they need not venture forward to the shadow of the chute. But it also brings to the cockpit extra control lines which will require understanding if everything is to go smoothly.

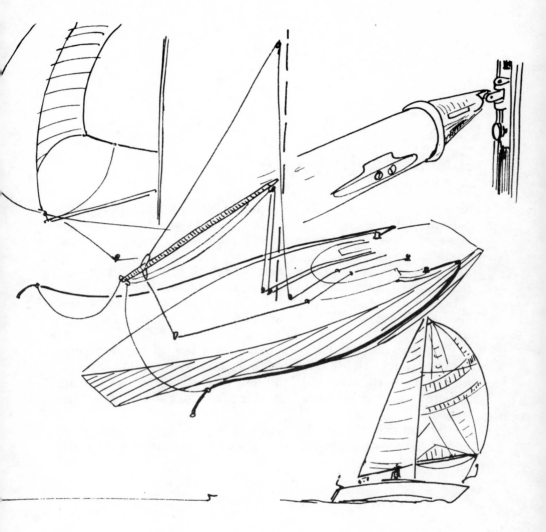

Twin Pole Gybe

This is necessary if the boat has an inner forestay or a baby stay, thus prohibiting the dip-pole system, and if you don't want to use the end-for-end method, which we have already seen can lead to trouble.

It means more hardware: two poles, two lifts, two guys, two mast cups. On the other hand, there is less 'knitting'.

Sheets and guys are permanently attached to the spinnaker. The pole is not clipped to the sheet in the normal way, but to the guy.

With the wind dead aft, the new pole is topped up and swung into position, with lift and downhaul trimmed. Easing the lift and downhaul on the other side, the clew is now released, so that the leeward pole can be stowed on deck after the mainsail has been gybed.

By hauling in the guy, the spinnaker is now drawn down to the end of the new pole, which may then be trimmed as usual.

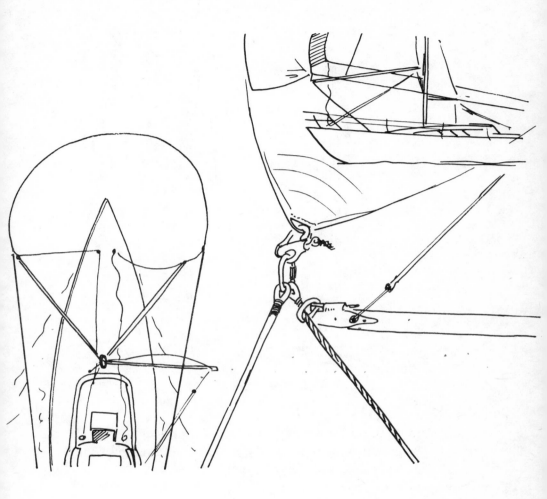

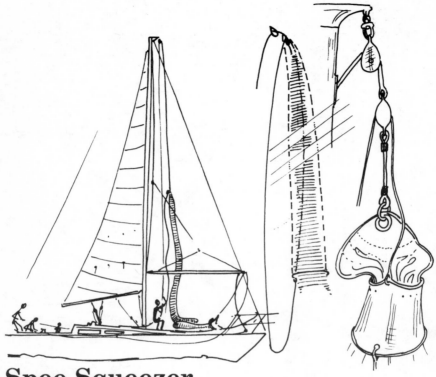

Spee Squeezer

The spinnaker chute, or tube, offers so many advantages that it could well become standard equipment on all day sailers and trailer boats. There is a development which seems to be even more interesting for cruising boats.

The spinnaker is rigged in a sheath or sleeve which has a hard bell mouth at its lower end. The sleeve has a block at the top, and is hoisted to the mast head; the block carries an endless halyard attached to the bell mouth, the upper part of which passes through the bell mouth itself.

When the sheathed sail has been hoisted, everything else is prepared on deck: guy, sheet, spinnaker pole etc. are all connected to the spinnaker clews which are hanging just clear of the bell mouth (Fig.1). When all is ready, the bell mouth is hauled to the head of the spinnaker (which the alert reader will remember is

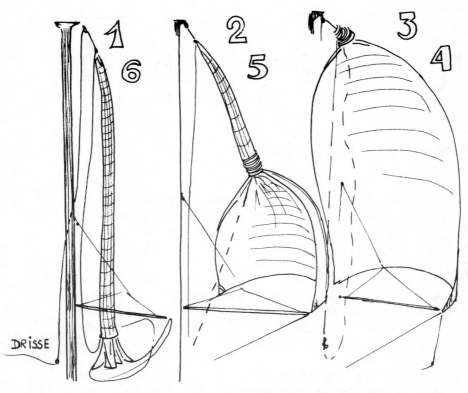

DRISSE

already at the mast head) and the sheath folds like a concertina (Figs. 2 and 3). There is little danger of a twist because, the top of the sail being the last to come out of the sheath, the spinnaker always fills from the foot (Fig.2).

Once the spinnaker has filled, the bell mouth control line is made fast to a cleat on the mast, and the spinnaker becomes just like any other — with the slight addition of the bell mouth and sheath aloft.

To furl it, the procedure is normal. The spinnaker pole is allowed to go forward to the stay, so that the sail can collapse in the lee of the mainsail. It may then be sheathed by pulling down on the bell mouth, which produces the sequence 4,5,6.

Now that the spinnaker is furled, smothered in its sheath, it can wait if there is something more important going on. After which the whole thing, spinnaker, sheath and bell mouth, is lowered, put in a sailbag and stowed in a locker.

71

Spinnaker Sally

Another sailmaker, mulling over the same problem, has replaced the sleeve by a series of plastic rings joined by a light line which keeps them equidistant on the furled spinnaker.

The master ring, which replaces the bell mouth of the Spee Squeezer, has a lug on which is fastened the control line.

This lug sees that the master ring is kept more or less at right angles to the axis of the spinnaker, and will run smoothly; the other rings then stack up properly on top of it.

The unfurling line is interlaced with the spacing lines which keep the rings evenly separated, thus contributing to their control.

The two systems shown almost completely eliminate problems of furling and unfurling the spinnaker. There's plenty of time to get everything ready at leisure — sheets, downhaul, pole, guys and lift can all be prepared and set for basic trim, since the spinnaker won't deploy until the bell mouth or master ring is hauled to the mast head.

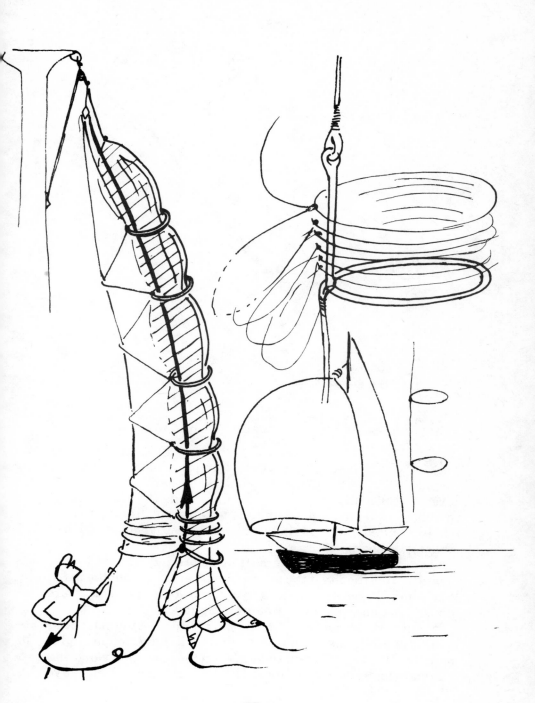

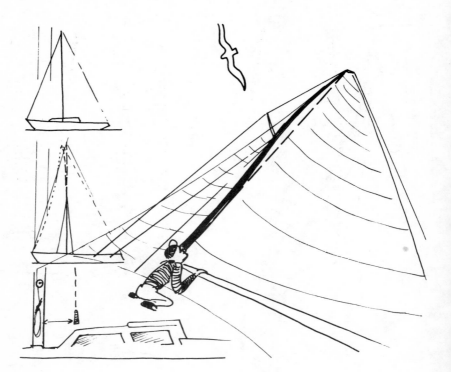

Tuning the Rig

The boatyard has stepped your mast. In principle, setting up the rigging is not part of their job — unless the contract specifically says so. It is really only while actually sailing that each item of rigging can be given the fine tune necessary, if the mast is to remain centred and straight (athwartships) as it should do when cruising or racing.

Apart from the question of mast rake, fore and aft trim doesn't present any difficulty if the main shrouds are abeam of the mast. If you have lowers or a baby stay you can reckon that they are properly set up when they are nicely tight.

In tuning the shrouds at rest, you can afford to let the mast head go a little aft. Under sail, tension on the jib halyard, plus a bit more from the forestay and some give on the backstay, will bring it forward to the correct position. Think about it if you do not have

74

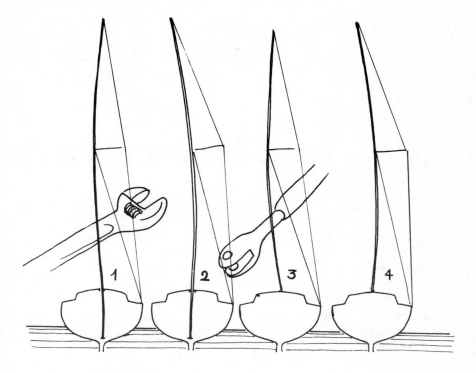

a tensioning tackle or some other sort of turnbuckle on the backstay.

Athwartships, the relative tension between lowers and cap shrouds must be right.

Through-deck Mast. In Fig. 1 the lowers are too slack, and the cap shroud might be a trifle tight if the mast is found to be pressing on the partners. In Fig. 2 the lowers are too tight and the cap shrouds too slack.

Deck-stepped Mast. In Fig. 3 the lowers are slack. Tighten them first, then check the cap shrouds again. In Fig. 4 the cap shrouds are too slack and the lowers may be too tight.

Tuning is a question of trial and error, with one adjustment at a time. Under all sail, sight up the mast track to see what the spar is doing. Set up the rig on each tack, one item at a time.

It is wise to check final settings carefully, marking the turnbuckles with nail varnish, or counting the screw threads showing.

Balance under Sail — Rigging

The rudder of a boat which carries a slight amount of weather helm helps resist leeway. But if the weather helm is too great, besides increasing drag, the helmsman becomes tired to the point where he or she will be less able to cope in emergency. The load can be reduced by the use of shock cord to carry some of it and, if the sails seem properly trimmed, by altering the rake of the mast.

The boatyard may not have established the correct rake, having been content simply to step the mast and tighten up the rigging all round. By adjusting the rake (even slanting the mast slightly forward), it is possible to alter the boat's balance under sail quite a lot. Bear in mind the old timers' saying 'A well balanced boat often has slight lee helm in light weather.'

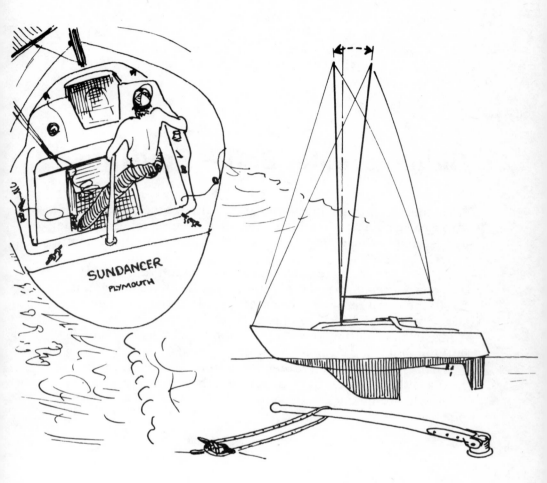

Balance under Sail — Sail Trim

A full mainsail, which may be ideal for light weather, will quickly give weather helm if the wind increases. Before reducing area, the sail trimmer should flatten the sail and bring the power-point nearer the mast.

This is done by increasing tension on the luff and foot. If the gooseneck runs on a track, it should be pulled hard down; if it is fixed, the same result can be obtained with a cunningham hole, which you should fit if you haven't got one.
You can also flatten the sail slightly by pulling on the clew outhaul, but the gear must be properly thought out.

When cruising I would rather spend time and effort in trying to increase the flow in a flat sail during light weather, rather than having to struggle to flatten one which is too full when the wind pipes up.

III   Safety

Side Netting

An attractive netting protection on the lifelines, with mesh small enough to stop a child slipping through, can be produced with a little patience — only the most rudimentary skill is required.

The lower fastenings need either eye straps on the toe-rail of a size to suit the line used or, which I prefer, installation of a third lifeline along the deck itself.

The net is made in two stages. Start by lacing the top line between the upper and intermediate lifelines. The easiest way is to pass the line around the middle lifeline, before taking it up to make a clove hitch on the upper rail and back to another turn round the intermediate (Fig. A).

Better looking, but needing care to work out the right length, is the system in Fig. B, where the net is not attached to the lifeline at the join, or that of Fig. C, where the two lacings are interlocked round the intermediate lifeline.

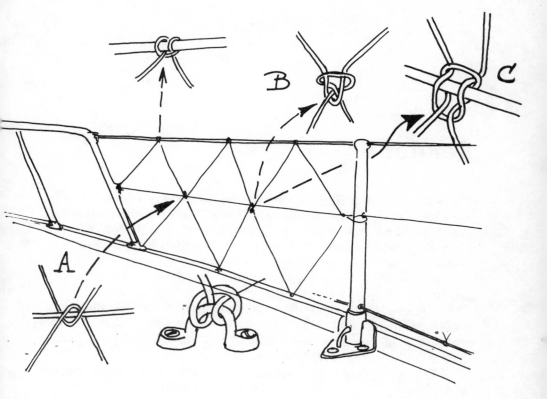

Fenders

There are certain things which the wise owner stows away when he reaches port, usually for fear of thieves. There are others which are stowed when putting to sea. Fenders are among the latter, but lockers are seldom big enough to hold ones which will give decent protection.

Quite a lot of boats carry scars which bigger fenders would have prevented. This is one of the occasions when 'big is beautiful'.

But where to put these nautical punchbags? Or how do you justify the space they take up?

Modern fenders float well. They can almost be considered as lifebelts — not official, but efficient (some are even bright orange). So it is not entirely inappropriate to have them somewhere on deck.

If there is an eye in their lashing, they can be strung from a single line; if there is one at each end, so much the neater. Or they make a soft seat if they are tied side by side on the coachroof.

They can also be stowed on the lifelines or the aft pulpit, as is frequently seen on power cruisers.

Spare Halyards

Some mastheads have two sheaves for each halyard. This means less wear for external halyards, but only leaves you with two: mainsail and headsail.

Sometimes two of these halyards use only one sheave each, and then lead inside the mast — usually the main and jib, the topping lift still using two sheaves and coming out in front of the mast again.

If the lift is stout enough, one end can then be used as an emergency jib halyard, the other for the main. Internal halyards cannot be used as spares unless there are spares as such.

For a long cruise, an extra sheave at the side of the masthead should be added if a spare halyard is wanted. A spinnaker halyard is a wise addition, even without the sail. Forward, this and the topping lift can back up the jib; aft, the lift can back up the mainsail.

It is difficult to gather an internal halyard which has escaped inside the mast, unless the exit hole is big enough to allow the doubled line to be hooked out.

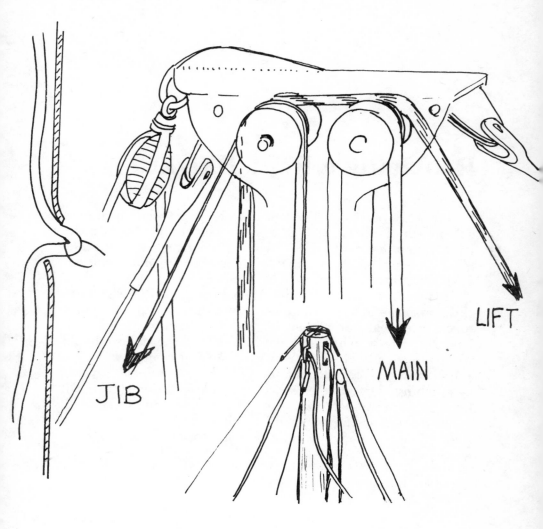

JIB

MAIN

LIFT

Replacing a Rope Halyard

Pre-stretched polyester (Terylene or Dacron) is becoming universal on small boats, and makes the best halyards. Periodic replacement, before they part (which of course means that they must be checked from time to time), can be done without unstepping the mast.

House removal firms use an extremely strong adhesive tape to close cartons and boxes. Wrapped round the two ends of braided rope, butted together, and supported by a few stitches, they will hold them firmly in line. The new halyard will thus follow the old without difficulty, and will reeve as the other comes away.

With laid rope, the old and new halyards can be held together by stitching alone. Two close whippings keep the ends tidy; sail twine is sewn through one strand, back to one on the other end, and so on back and forth. When the three strands have been sewn, a second series of holding stitches is made as with a sailmaker's whipping.

Small Safety Items

Harnesses, fire extinguishers, flares, radar reflector, signalling flashlight, reefing lines etc. should all be stowed readily to hand — and whereabouts known to everybody.

These small items nearly always end up by being pushed to the bottom of a drawer or locker, forced back by other gear more frequently in use.

It is better to have a separate stowage. There are several possibilities.

Fig. A. Fastened to the lid of a cockpit locker and/or in a sealed bag on the end of an attached line.

Fig. B. Certain emergency tools can be fitted by shock cord under the steps of the companion ladder.

Fig. C. The companion ladder also makes a good place to tie a 'panic bag'.

Fig. D. Flashlight, fire extinguishers and flares will be right to hand on the inside of the aft saloon bulkhead.

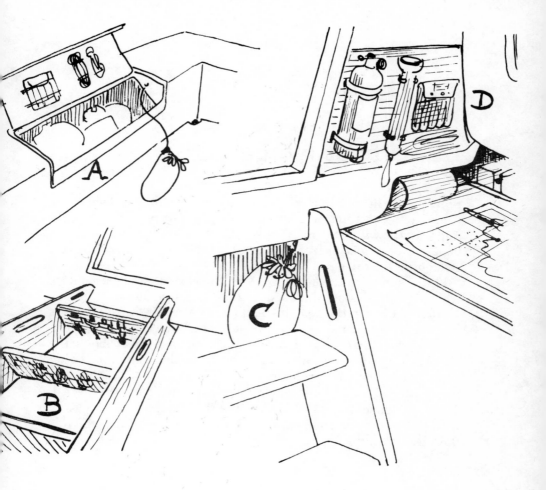

Liferaft Stowage

Stowing the liferaft in a small boat is a real headache, if space for it has not been thought of by the designer. At best it looks ugly and is in the way; at worst it blocks the view or interferes with the boom vang. It also encroaches heavily on the spot where you can stretch out in the sun.

I have shown in the upper drawing the various standard places where it can be stowed, depending on deck layout.

Having chosen the spot, it should have a cradle so that it stays put yet, at the same time, can be launched quickly.

Two systems are shown: one on the deck with six eyebolts; the other if there are lateral fixtures such as the coachroof being extended forward on each side.

In both cases the lashings are not taken right round the liferaft. They are tensioned, as shown in the drawing, by a cross strap with an eye at one end running on one of the lashings, which is then hauled tight and tied with a slip knot.

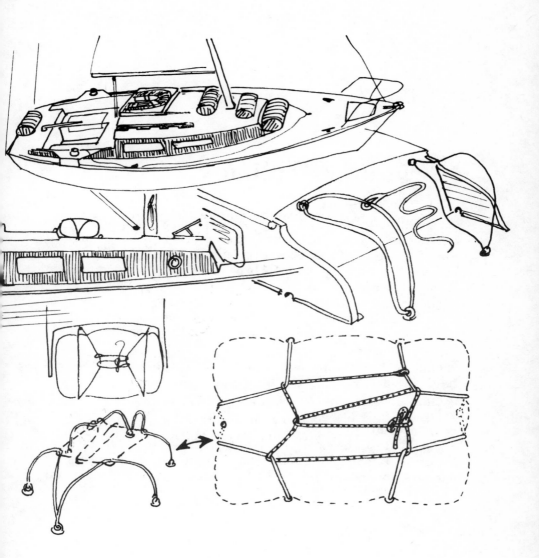

Horseshoe Lifebuoy

On small boats there's no knowing what to do with the lifebuoy. It often ends up in an inaccessible corner, where it has gradually been pushed, perhaps because there is no aft pulpit, or else because the one fitted just fails to be tall enough to accommodate it with its emergency light.

The horseshoe lifebuoy can, however, be stowed where it will be both readily available and unobtrusive if some care is taken.

Fig. A. On the transom, perhaps astride the tiller if the latter's movement is not too great.

Fig. B. On the after deck, behind the cockpit, attached to a hatch or vent to stop it moving about.

Fig. C. On the main hatch.

Fig. D. If the cockpit lockers are deep, it can be given a special compartment.

Fig. E. It can be easily fitted to the span of the backstay.

Fig. F. It should be ready for instant use. This means no cumbersome lashings to undo, but shock cord, with toggle and eye.

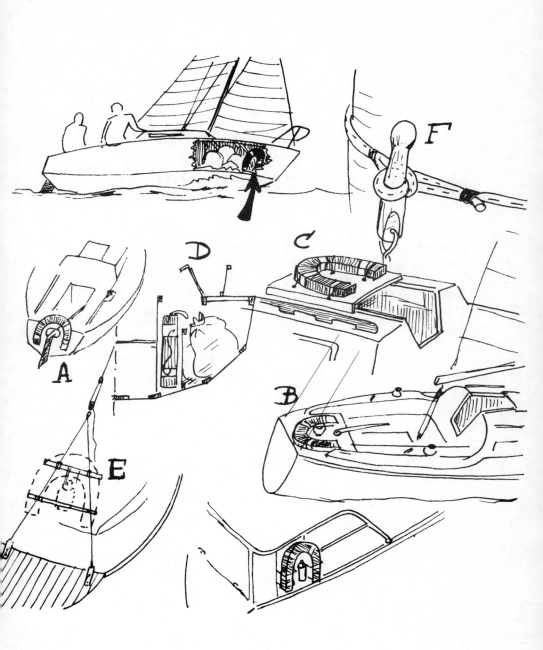

Safety of Safety Equipment

The liferaft — a costly item — which must be capable of easy launching while sailing, should also be protected from the covetous attentions of dockside thieves.

If it is in the aft seat locker — a convenient place on many small boats — use of the lid lock shown above will avoid having to take it below at each stop.

This lid of ⅜in ply will lift right off when necessary, but it can be locked as soon as it is closed; a simple padlock is enough Naturally, the plates and hinges should be bolted and burred over, not fastened with screws.

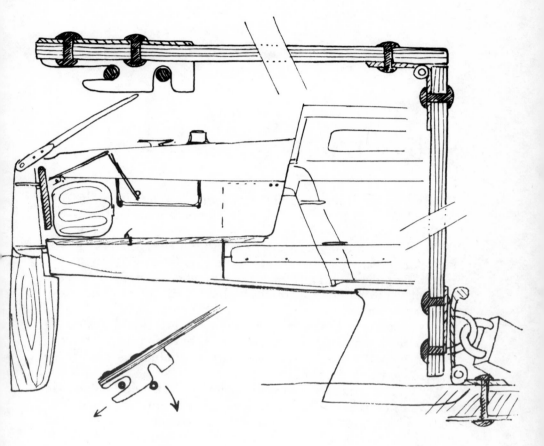

Safety Lines

Each crewman should be able to hook on his safety harness from the cockpit, and then proceed to the foredeck without further re-hooking.

This means having a safety line, either a permanent stainless steel wire or a temporary pre-stretched polyester rope (⅜in dia, 1¼ in circ) rigged tightly from a strongpoint just forward of the cockpit to another on the foredeck (the mooring cleat or sampson post for example).

It is easier to haul a member of the crew who is hanging over the side on his harness line back on board, if he or she doesn't have to be got over the lifelines. Pelican hooks enable the rails to be broken and closed again easily.

The solo mariner will not want to don lifejacket and harness in fine weather. A length of line trailing astern, which he can grab if he falls overboard, may represent the difference between life and death. If it is made fast to the tiller, to leeward, grabbing it will make the boat luff and then gybe, thereby slowing the boat and also alerting anyone below that something is amiss.

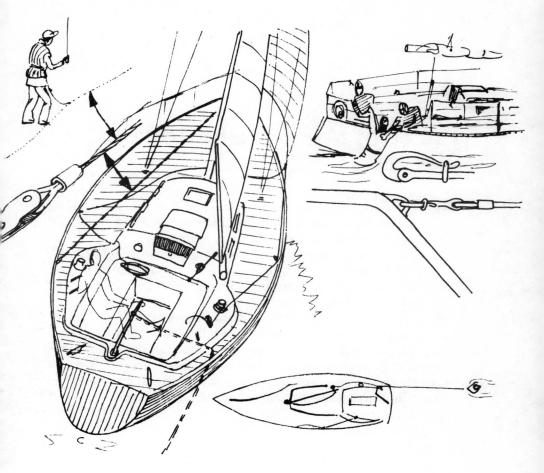

Peace of Mind in Shallow Waters

The echo sounder is usually installed with the other electronic instruments near the chart table, so that the navigator can see it, and to keep it sheltered from the elements.

In some cases it is impossible to fit a repeater dial, and, unless a crewman is banished below to call out the readings, the helmsman will thus be deprived of information which may be important when feeling his way in shallow waters.

By mounting the indicator on the aft bulkhead, on a hinged bracket next to the companion way, it will be possible to swing the dial to face the helmsman, so that he can get along without this extra help. Because the main hatch is a regular thoroughfare, it is worth rigging some form of shock cord arrangement to hold the bracket in position but so that it can be easily moved.

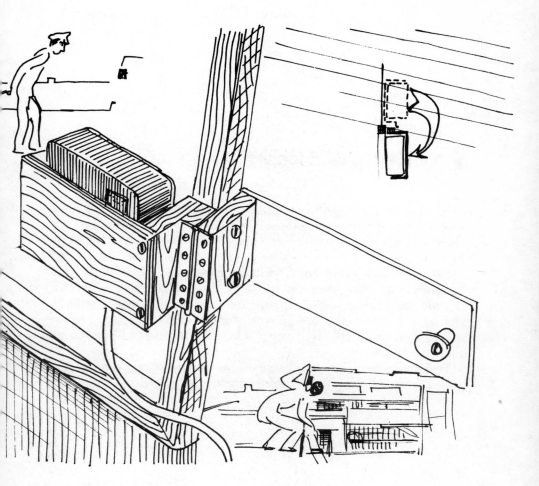

Pulpits and Lifelines

Even though leaving the cockpit to go onto the weather deck may be easy, the reverse process invites disaster, all the more likely if the grab rails on the coachroof are calf level or even, at best, knee height.

Lifelines on a small boat, while both required by the rules and reassuring in port, are more likely to hinder than help when the boat is heeled. Having often admired the idea of a taffrail round the base of the mast to help working there in big boats, I have adapted the principle by having a kind of pulpit installed round the main hatch.

I now regain my cockpit in peace; in addition I can rig a shade over the open hatch if the weather gets really hot.

Reducing the Volume

Huge cockpits, which are fine for fishing, are not so good in day sailers converted from fishing smacks, because of the large proportion of the boat's useful volume which they represent.

The seakeeping qualities of these boats are usually excellent, and the facilities which have been added to some of them make them good for cruising. The problem remains that there is always a risk of meeting one big sea which could swamp the boat in seconds.

This open volume can be limited fairly easily by use of air bags, provided they are properly secured. This implies the use of eyebolts able to withstand the Archimedes force which will try to dislodge them when submerged (A), rather than screwed fastenings.

They will go nicely into the aft end of the cockit, under a solid panel firmly battened down on top (B). Make sure that any cockpit drains are not blocked.

Lengths of plastic piping, as used by house plumbers, make useful spacers if fitted under the inflated buoyancy bags.

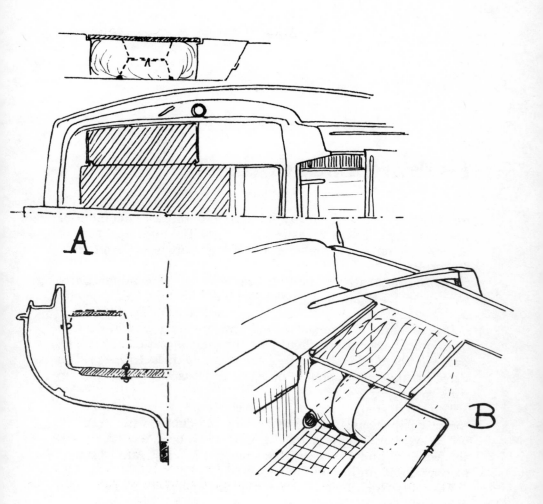

A

B

Bathing Ladder

Strange as it may seem, in my opinion the bathing ladder is one of the most useful safety measures on board. The high freeboard of modern cruising boats means that it has more uses than purely for bathing.

Getting on board from an inflatable is not too easy for many women, or for those men who are a bit on the flabby side, or who may be carrying a lot of gear for that matter.

It is also difficult to get a tired crew member who has fallen overboard back into the boat without some assistance. For this purpose, the ladder should be somewhere near the transom. The three arrangements shown opposite are practical and take up little room.

Top left, a step is mounted on the rudder blade with another on the transom itself. It is always ready and causes little drag.

The one to the right is quite useful. It pivots on a bolt through the transom, and was built from a piece of ¾in ply. A fixed step is also mounted higher up the transom.

The last, which I saw for the first time on a Swedish boat, also closes off the aft pulpit and can be lowered to allow stern-on marina access.

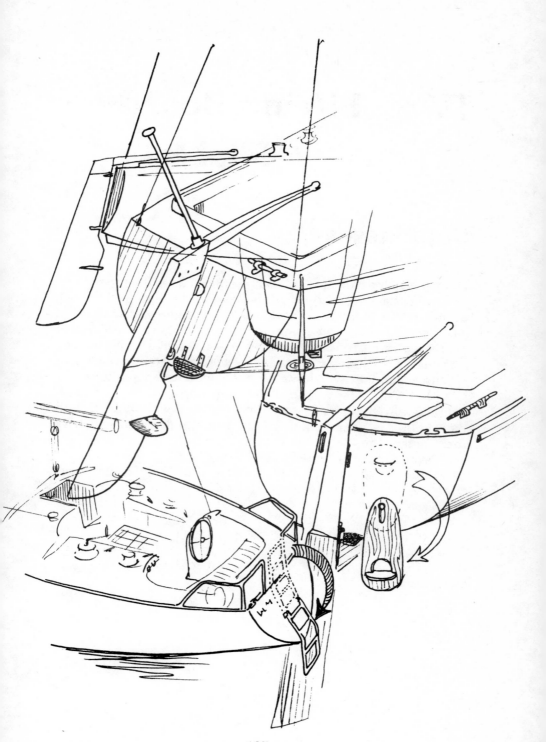

IV   Life on Board

Sunglasses

I haven't made this up — it really happened.

We were cruising as a crew of six, all of whom were middle aged, all fairly long-sighted so that we only wore glasses for reading; each one of us also had a pair of sunglasses. This made a total of twelve pairs either being used or lying about the place. The weather was glorious, so that we were not wearing a lot of clothing, and that which we did have on, had few pockets.

Rather than resign ourselves to spending days on end in fruitless search, we made a rack by pleating a wide band of cloth more or less to the sizes shown at the top of the drawing, which we then fastened to a plywood board.

It revolutionised our lives. . .

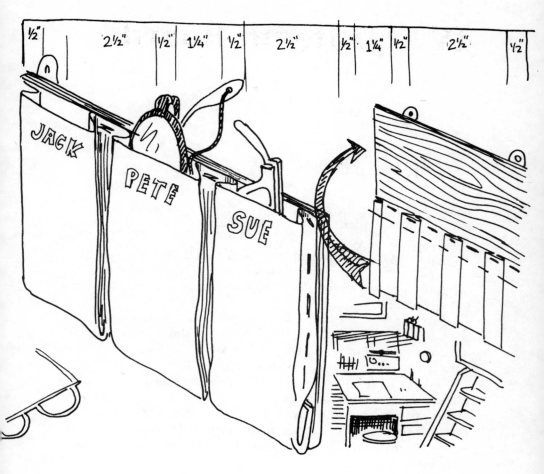

Makeshift Pillow

Small boats aren't very big. . . Their size, such as it may be, is entirely independent of that of the crews who sail in them. Although one is constantly being astonished to see what can be stowed away, these two truths remain, and there must be a limit.

Sacrifices must therefore be made, among the first of which is often the pillow belonging to the spare bunk, which often turns out to be mine.

I have solved the problem by a double stowing of my gear. Sweaters aren't folded but rolled, as I have shown opposite; they are then stowed in a soft bag with a velcro fastening, which in turn is put into a normal dunnage bag.

If I don't have enough personal locker space, or I haven't got a pillow, my sweaters remain in their soft bag to do a double duty under my head at night. Even with a decent locker, rolling them makes it possible to get at whatever is wanted without disturbing the rest of my gear. This system is so convenient that I even use it at home in the house.

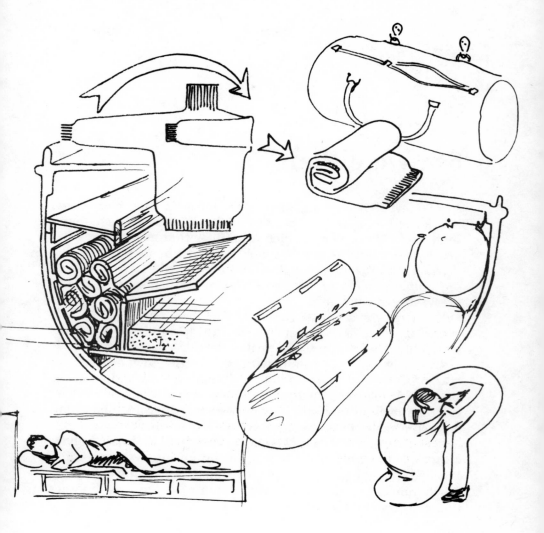

Stowage Plan

After a few days cruising, most of the miscellaneous gear which was loaded on board at the start of the season will have found some niche or corner, in such a manner that everything — or nearly everything — can be quickly found when wanted.

When the season is over, the boat is emptied and laid up, and the winter is spent thinking of other things; the following spring everything starts again.

The first days at sea are often spoiled by either having endlessly to search for, or else replace (possibly both), items which have been only temporarily mislaid.

A detailed stowage plan, with numbered stowages, odd to starboard, even to port (followed, if you have a mind for these things, by letters indicating the level above the keel and by figures showing the distance from the centreline of the boat) can make life easier by showing exactly what is where.

If you can do it when laying up, empty all lockers, shelves, hanging cupboards and drawers, one by one into boxes carefully labelled with the place its contents came from. Fitting out will be much quicker, and you'll avoid having to buy yet another unnecessary sailing hat or splicing tool.

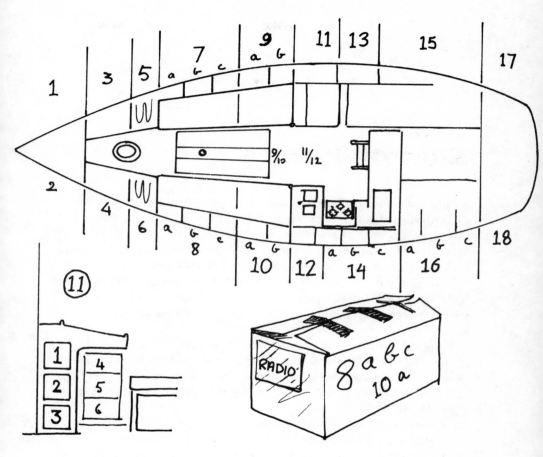

'Cathedral' Berths

A high freeboard, which produced such wonderful interior volume some time back, also produced berths with cathedral-like proportions.

In view of the perpetual shortage of adequate lockers, it seems sensible to look for ways of using this 'lost' volume if you have this kind of old-fashioned vessel. Enough room must, of course, be left to stretch out on your back, with knees raised. Anything which exceeds this height (1ft 8in above the mattress) is fair game.

There are several possible solutions, but access to the end of a long locker as in Fig. A is not always easy. Installation of a large drawer, with its attendant runners, may be beyond the average handyman. I have found the hinged tray shown in Fig. B to be very practical.

Dividers across the tray help keep things tidy. It is closed by a bolt, a cord or a jam cleat.

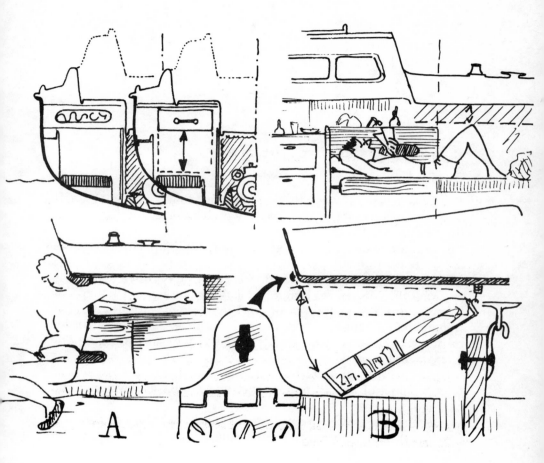

A

B

Extra Sea Berths

The fo'cs'le is not always the most comfortable of places at sea. It is often cluttered with wet sailbags which have to be shifted when the berths need to be used.

If the saloon coachroof height is enough, pilot berths of canvas are quite comfortable.

For this purpose there should be 3ft 6in clearance above the main berth. The canvas is made fast along one side (with hooks or lacing eyes) and supported along the other by an alloy tube or wooden pole. This should be adjustable in three positions, in order to make a berth which is wide and flat when at moorings or narrow and deep when at sea.

It will be nice and warm, even underneath, if a ¼in sheet of foam or part of an old foam duvet or coverlet is sewn into the canvas.

The bunk is stowed by rolling it round the tube or pole, and either lashing it against the cabin side, or else removing it to the fo'cs'le.

Overhangs and Other Distant Places

I saw this for the first time long ago, on a Dragon belonging to some friends who used her for cruising, despite her lack of amenities. It was important that nothing should be stowed in the main cabin, because all three of us slept there (one on the cabin sole between the bunks).

To fetch something from the overhangs entailed acrobatics which were all the more unwelcome, because it was rare that the other two could resist the temptation to pinch a defenceless posterior.

A couple of blocks fastened to the sampson post made it easy to haul dunnage bags up to the bow to be stowed; another line enabled them to be pulled back to the cabin. Both operations could be done sitting down. . .

I remembered this idea when I needed to use this space underneath my cockpit, in order to stow the three spare lifejackets I keep for guests when not needed. The blocks are mounted on a board which pushes under the cockpit and then jams against the end of the cabin floorboards.

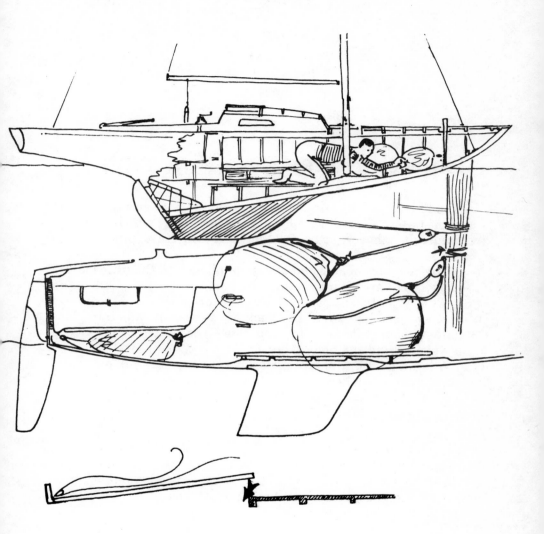

Locker Boxes

It is always hard to find stowage which is both secure, and yet immediately accessible, for tools or other items which might be needed in a hurry: spare flashlight, reefing lines, pipe, tobacco etc.

The companion steps make a good place, and the little lockers shown here are an interesting solution.

When it is stacked, with the lip of its forward face in the groove and against the stop at the back of the step, it falls into place automatically. It stays there because the centre of gravity is always behind the pivot point.

A hand-hold in the face makes it easy to slot it into place and also to carry it wherever it may be needed.

Fresh Water

To fill the water tank ashore often entails waiting for the hose, or even for the water to be turned on at the mains. Anything which can help economise on fresh water will be useful. The following may be considered.

Fig. A. A separate circuit breaker for the water pump.

Fig. B. A direct pump to return to the tank any fresh water which has to be run cold before it warms up from the heater.

Fig. C. A salt water pump to the sink — sea water lathers perfectly well with modern detergents. Fresh water is kept for a final rinse after the dishes have been washed clean in salt water.

Fig. D. A foot pump rather than a hand pump, because then both hands can be washed at the same time.

Fig. E. An on/off cock installed between the pump and the sink or basin, and kept almost shut; a diaphragm on the outlet itself only lets through an adequate dribble of water, not a deluge.

Fig. F. A small container with a little tap or faucet will combine everything on really small boats (I have drawn a home-modified hot water bottle here).

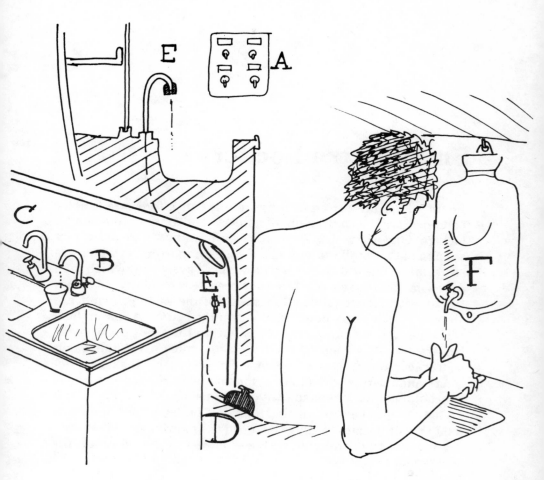

Small Extra Lockers

Boats which are priced at a figure one can afford, are usually equipped with a minimum of joinery and only a few simple lockers. One or two big lockers are built in, but there are rarely enough of the small individual stowage compartments which are so useful for the little items which are used every day, which then take some finding unless they have been very carefully put away.

To meet this need, two applications of the same principle are shown, which is to make use of small plastic basins or food containers. They can be fitted easily into the lid of under-berth lockers (A). The hole is cut just large enough for the basin concerned, and it rests on a frame screwed inside the locker lid. There should be a gap to allow for the basin rim, or else a new wooden insert can be made out of thinner ply.

One can also be fitted behind a vertical bulkhead (B), alongside a bunk, if it is made of plywood, or in the part bulkhead separating a bunk from the galley area — access is then through the permanent opening.

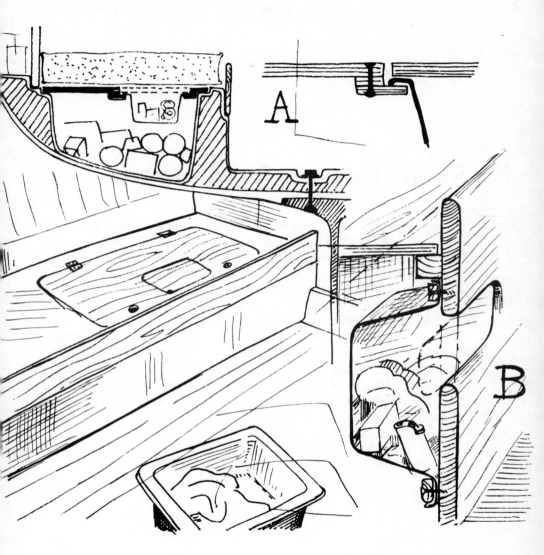

Small Items in Big Lockers

Plastic cockpits lack individual stowage spaces, so that small items get put into big lockers and then get lost.

It is easy to fit a small plastic box (ice cream containers are good) under the locker lid, for such small items. It should be hinged outboard near to the hinges of the lid itself. Closed by turn-buttons at the cockpit side, short straps hold it open at a convenient level when the locker lid is raised.

It is sometimes possible, though less convenient, to fit a drawer underneath the seat or deck, astern or ahead of the lid, if waterproofing can be assured by a compression joint as used to be common in the 'good old days'; or else, if the lid has side screens, then the drawer must be fitted between the locker and the main planking at the side of the boat.

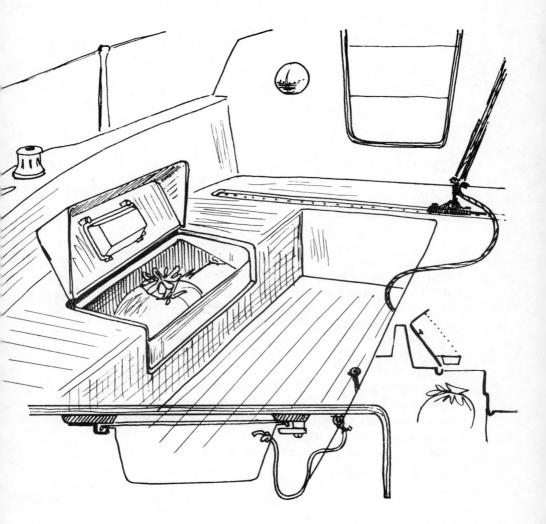

More Lockers

Man gets bigger, and quite a lot of crewmen these days complain that bunks are too short. The builder tries to pack too much into a small hull. But not everyone is big, and not everyone sleeps as I do, with one arm stretched above his head.

A friend of mine, who sleeps practically doubled up, worked out that he could knock eight inches off his bunk all round, without being over the edge. So he decided to fit three drawers under the armrest at the head of the berth (I suspect that he only decided to do it because it is one of the few places on board where nice looking fittings can be added without too many curves and bevels).

* The top one is reserved for knives, forks, spoons and sundry other galley items.

* The bottom one is full of tools, blocks, spare shackles (with and without pins) and the like.

* The one in the middle is for general crew use (sunglasses, knives, cameras etc.).

V Ventilation

Upper and Lower Ventilation

The switch from what is now called the 'classical' construction in wood has eliminated most of the dangers brought on by lack of proper ventilation. Modern boats made of plastic, alloy or steel don't rot.

There are, however, certain boats which nevertheless smell of mildew. So, good ventilation remains important. But it is not always easy to arrange, as a look round any Boat Show will quickly reveal.

Damp and stale air must always be avoided. If not already incorporated, doors which close off hanging lockers, and all lockers proper, should have vents both high and low — simple holes drilled in the sides, or hand-holds in the lids will do the trick.

If the hull isn't insulated, a lining of some sort will stop clothes getting wet from condensation running down the sides.

When laying up, all lockers and floorboards should be opened up so that air can circulate.

More Ventilation

A few fresh air reminders may be worth setting down. 'Natural' ventilation occurs from the stern towards the bow — don't ask me why. It is rarely enough on modern boats designed to be comfortable even in warm wet weather. Without too much effort, the following can be incorporated.

Fig. A. If there is a cabin locker next to the fore cabin, a vent box or proprietory ventilation mushroom can be sited on top of it — depending on the position of cleats and the run of the anchor chain. The chain locker becomes the baffle, and those in the forecabin will welcome the fresh air.

Fig. B. There are ready made ventilation boxes of the Dorade type, but it is not always easy to decide where to place them.

Fig. C. Easier and less cumbersome is the extractor, comprising a simple sheet of flexible neoprene held in a metal frame screwed to the deck, and covering an opening which has been properly waterproofed — as should be all those mentioned above.

Fig. D. Main hatch door louvres are nice to look at, but not often found these days due to their expense.

Fig. E. Lacking that, a wild sleeve fixed over the fore hatch and held up by the spinnaker pole topping lift, is easy to rig and works well in harbour.

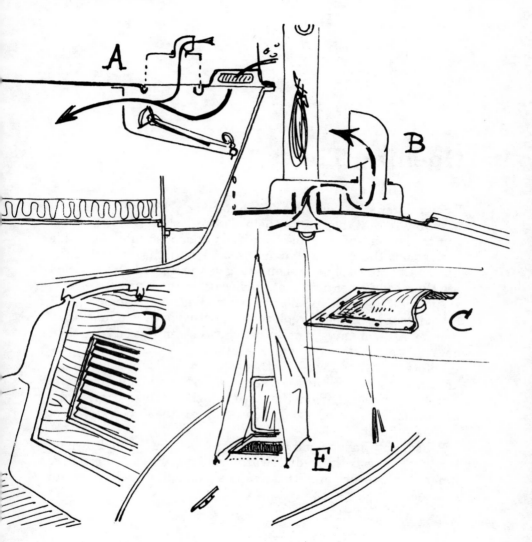

Opening Times

I don't know why, but most fore hatches are hinged forward — probably so that they will be helped to keep shut by rain squalls. But these don't often come from dead ahead, so that they slide insiduously through any gap in the sides, with the result that the hatch is slammed shut as soon as it gets the slightest bit wet. You are thus poorly ventilated at anchor or on the marina, because even a half-open lid doesn't make a very good extractor.

Last year I decided to replace mine with one which hinged aft, thereby assuring myself of far better cabin ventilation from then on, much appreciated in warm weather.

Before that I had found another solution, no doubt well enough known but which I have not seen used often. It consisted quite simply of anchoring from the stern, which put the cockpit in the best draft and allowed a good flow of air into the saloon by way of the main hatch.

Reasonably easy to add to a modern boat, the hatch drawn on the right may be hinged forward or aft at will, on alternative hinges which work on keyed shafts such as are used by certain shackles.

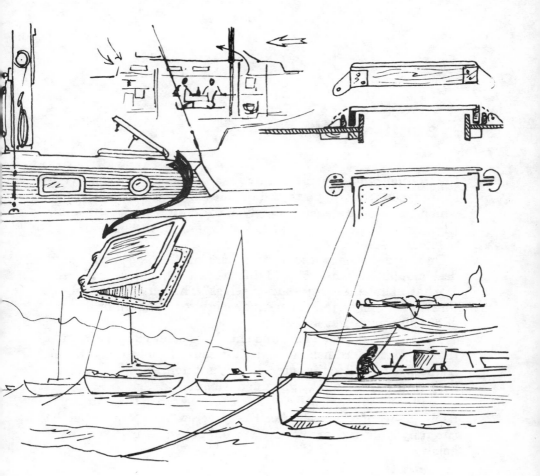

Hatch Vents

Ventilation problems only really assert themselves when flying spray means that all ports and hatches have to be closed. A box which can assure a steady supply of fresh air, without the water which might otherwise want to accompany it, will obviously be appreciated.

On a modern boat with sandwich construction and complicated deck mouldings, where should this magnificent object be placed?

What about the hatches themselves? The acrylic covering is flat, solid enough to support the weight of a crewman and, in addition, easy to cut and shape.

The box is made of wood, and should be screwed and sealed to the top with round head screws. It is sensible to ensure that the frame is extended to the outer rim of the hatch, so that the acrylic isn't called upon to take too much weight.

Loss of light below will not be great if the top of the vent box is itself made of clear acrylic. Every screw and joint must be carefully waterproofed, if only air and not water is to be carried below.

Ventilation in Port

Who hasn't at one time or another left a hatch open to air the boat during a short run ashore, only to find on return the results of a sharp rain squall?

A lump of sugar, doing the job of a fuse in a line holding the hatch open, would have avoided such a wetting.

The system is rather more efficient if the retaining line is long and near vertical, because drops of rain will collect and run down to the sugar more quickly, thereby melting it sooner.

I have also used this principle with success on a sliding hatch: a similarly 'fused' line is rigged to prevent a length of shock cord from closing it. The delay will be reduced if a third line is introduced into the system, running from the boom down to the sugar to increase the water supply and accelerate the melting process.

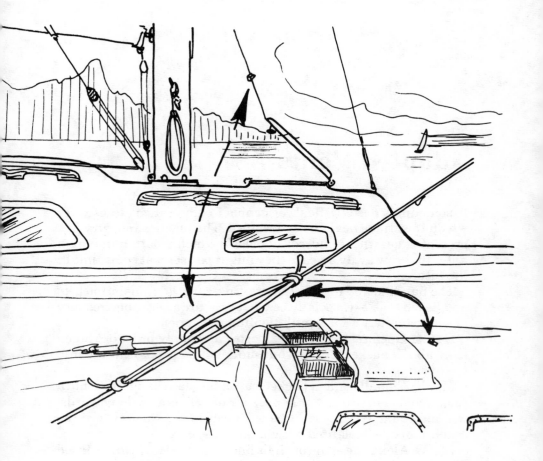

Adapted Vents

It sometimes needs a flash of genius to adapt items to uses for which they have never been designed. The plastics industry has presented us with hundreds of objects which a born handyman hates to throw away, in case they might be useful at some time in the future.

The hundred and one containers, tins, cans, lids plastic buckets and beach toys — especially beach toys — are a veritable treasury of source material for ventilation improvemnent.

Fig. A. Opening rectangular ports can supply or let out much more air if a bucket of somewhat similar dimensions is forced into the opening.

Fig. B. A small conical bucket, cut on the slant and forced into a round porthole, will not only pass air but, if pointed downwards, will also enable the port to be left open in the rain, even if the coachroof side is slanted outwards.

Fig. C. Along the same push fit lines, an air sleeve can be fitted to a hatch, if the bottom is stiffened by a frame which is just too big to pass through the hatch opening.

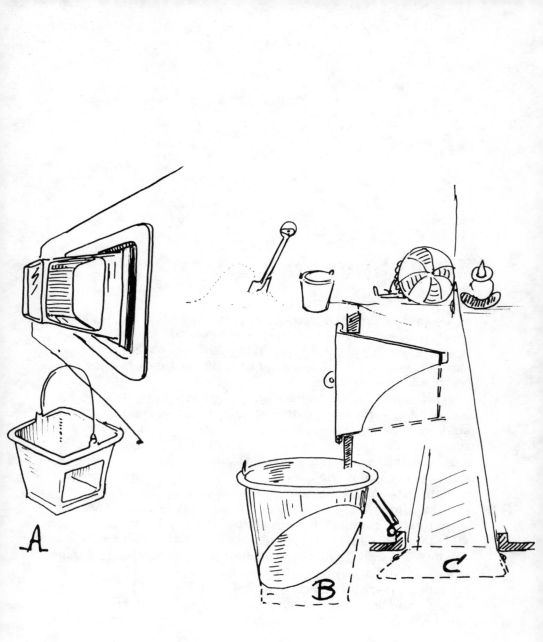

A

B

C

139

Small Boat Ventilation

Space problems, are of course, greatest on small boats, because space itself is limited in every sense of the word. It is not possible to provide room for everything which ought to be on deck, and still leave the crew room to stretch out from time to time — unless you resort to ingenuity again.

Ventilation trouble really starts when you have to close all hatches and ports, because this usually means no fresh air of any kind. The solution shown opposite really took my fancy.

The Dorade vent box is fixed to the main hatch itself, and is only used when the hatch is shut. It is made of ¼ in ply, and its shape is such that the horseshoe lifebuoy lies round it snugly (which thus finds a nice home for itself).

Only the two air tubes through the hatch cover need be watertight. It is quite OK to accept poor joinery between the box and the hatch, and it is not essential that the fit be flush because it can be made watertight by proprietory sealants etc.; half a dozen screws will hold it down.

I have drawn the device as I saw it: it is evident that a few inches could be saved in overall height by using swivelling PVC vents as sold in most good chandlers.

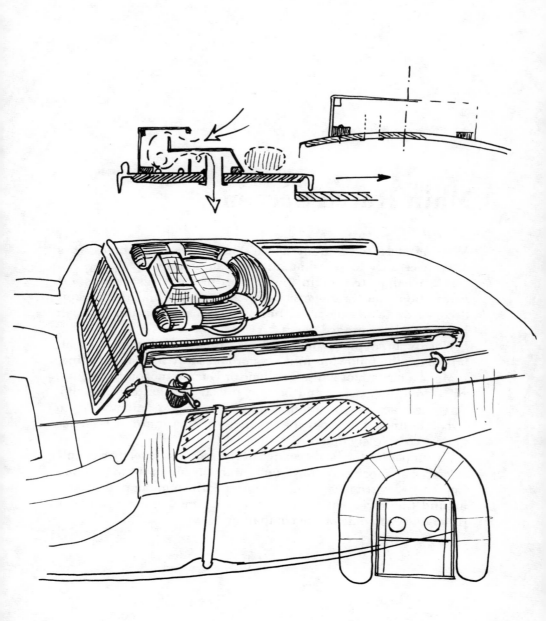

Main Hatch Screen

Mooring stern to the quay doesn't only have advantages. It is often necessary to guard against idle sightseers.

But closing the main hatch for privacy also shuts off ventilation, and passage between the saloon and the cockpit becomes quite an exercise if the hatch is closed by separate wash boards and not hinged doors.

Worthy of a place in this book, because it overcomes all problems, the following hint was produced by a friend of mine.

Make a curtain of white Terylene or Dacron mosquito netting, with broad hems top and bottom into which battens are slid. Stretched across the main companion way it allows air to circulate and, if lit from the inside by a spot lamp, it becomes almost completely opaque.

The upper batten is suspended at the required level by a couple of pieces of shock cord; push on it and you can move in and out. Control of length is effected by choosing the number of turns left around the lower batten, before it is jammed under two hooks fitted one each side of the companion way.

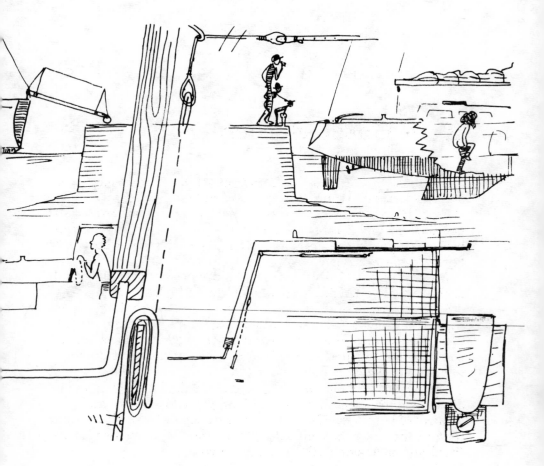

VI   The Galley

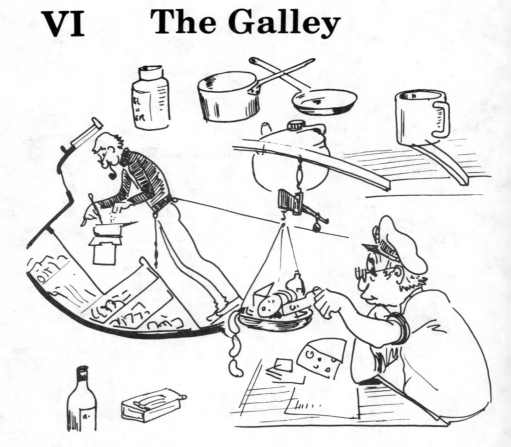

Cooking at Sea

The cook is one of the most important members of a cruising crew. As soon as the average deckhand gets his (or her) sea-legs, he seems to change into a bottomless food receptacle, a gannet who is only content as long as solid meal follows solid meal with unfailing regularity. His motto could well be 'One hand for the ship and one for the spoon.'

This transformation highlights the importance of two members of the crew: the one who is responsible for provisioning the ship with victuals and rations, and the one who knows how to make

best use of them in the galley — which is not always the same person, nor indeed is it easy at sea.

Even if you don't go in for deep water cruising, with its attendant daily catering problems, a passage along the coast can mean two or three meals at sea. A small galley is not always best designed for preparing big, hot meals in a choppy sea.

In effect, it is only a regular task for a fairly small number of cruising boats. Most people sail in hops, from port to port, and it becomes a matter of sandwiches, salads prepared in advance, cheese and fruit at noon, and often a visit to a cafe in the evening if it has been a tiring day. At sea, the cook only lights up the stove in anger in fine weather, or else perhaps when at anchor in the evening because it's quicker or cheaper.

Because boats are designed for Mr Average, it is natural that their galleys should be equally average. I hope that some of the ideas which follow will help make them that little bit more personal.

Shelf Security

Galley lockers are provided with fiddles of varying heights which are designed to stop a deluge of sauce bottles, packets of tea, beer cans and a host of other foodstuffs cascading out every time the boat heels sharply.

High fiddles hold everything firmly in place, but small packets can't be seen and it can be difficult to extract big ones. Low fiddles, and small objects can be seen OK but big ones fall out.

Fiddles which are removable (A) or plexiglass (C) or which are formed by transparent sliding doors (B) are ideas which are fairly common. The solution which seems best to me, and easy to instal, consists of fitting shock cord, at a fairly high level. It will hold the heaviest jar without having to be stretched too tight, if you run it behind vertical wires from top to bottom of the shelf. These must, of course, be far enough apart to allow the widest jar or container to pass — 4 to 6 inches is usually enough (D).

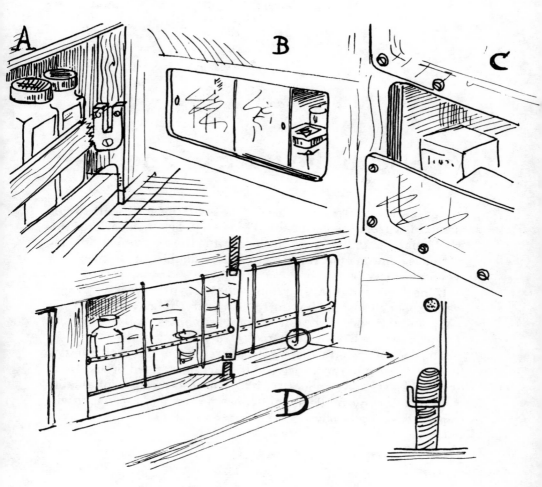

Access to the Back of Shelves

If the galley shelves are deep, it is sometimes difficult to get something from the very back. Things will be much easier if the shelf space is split between the locker and the door which closes it off, as is done on most refrigerators. This doubles the frontage, as you might say (A).

If the door swings three or four inches above the work surface, it can be opened without having to clear everything away each time (A1), and the front of the lowest compartment is easily accessible because the shelf above it is recessed.

The door of a shelf which is some three or four feet long is best if it hinges down to the horizontal (B). A stout hinged bracket arm will hold it strongly enough for it to be used as an occasional table or worktop. Any fiddle should cause no trouble, because it will normally be well above the contents as it shuts.

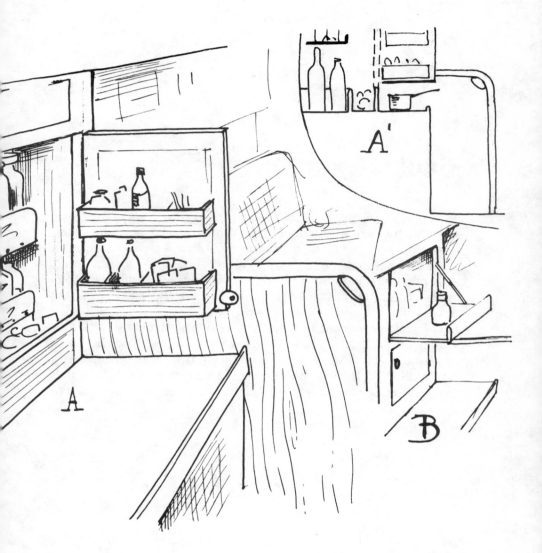

Fiddles

High fiddles are important if everything is to stay on the table at sea, but they are a nuisance when not in use. They add to the space taken up by a folding table, and they have awkward corners if you fall against them.

All of which no doubt explains why the average fiddle is rather smaller than it might be, so that it gets in the way less even if it is not so efficient.

So I looked for, and found, improvements. Removable fiddles (which, of course, then have to be stowed), fiddles which fold into a recess in the table (which are both fascinating and complicated); but chiefly the folding fiddles I have shown at the left (which leave the table completely free and flat at the marina, just like home).

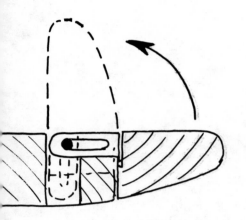

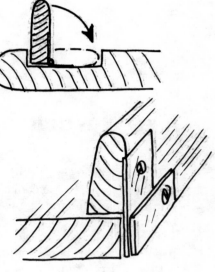

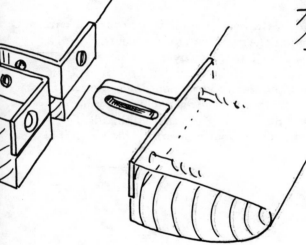

Extra Worktops

The galley of a small cruising boat is usually not well endowed with worktops. Some cooks make out very well and don't seem to mind, but a little more space will not come amiss, and it can often be provided.

The cover which goes over the cooker when it is not in use can become a worktop over a bunk (A), or it can hinge over the top of a settee to give more area (B). The sink cover can be a sliding worktop if the tap or faucet is carefully sited (C). And finally, the door of the locker nearest the galley can open down instead of being hinged sideways (D). It can even be replaced by a more imaginative arrangement resting on the part bulkhead, if this won't be too clumsy and make the seat uncomfortable when it is closed.

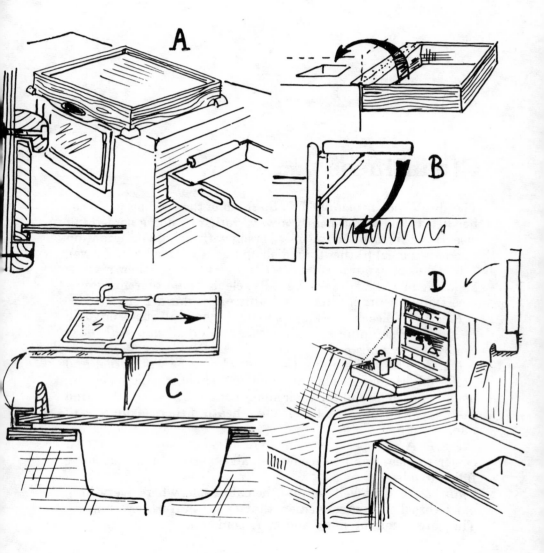

Cleanliness

The ship's cook is usually only there out of the goodness of his or her heart, and would nearly always rather be doing something else. He or she is often the only person with enough imagination to create a meal (rather than dish up a series of hashes or stews).

It is thus only fair that the rest of the crew (among them myself) should lend a hand to keep the galley clean. I have therefore given a certain amount of attention to this particular activity.

Fig. A. Fiddles on worktops should not be continuous or you'll be for ever scraping out the corners; a small gap will make removal of crumbs easier.

Fig. B. The space under the stove should be waterproof and preferably rounded: pots and pans on a stove, gimballed or not, usually finish by spilling their sticky contents ... which then find their way into the deep locker underneath if there is any sort of gap.

Fig. C. A bag specially made to fit under the stove will make it easier to clean, and to recover small objects which may have fallen inside.

Fig. D. A 'dust-well' let into the cabin sole, where everything can be brushed, is so convenient that it needs no further comment. They are becoming more and more common.

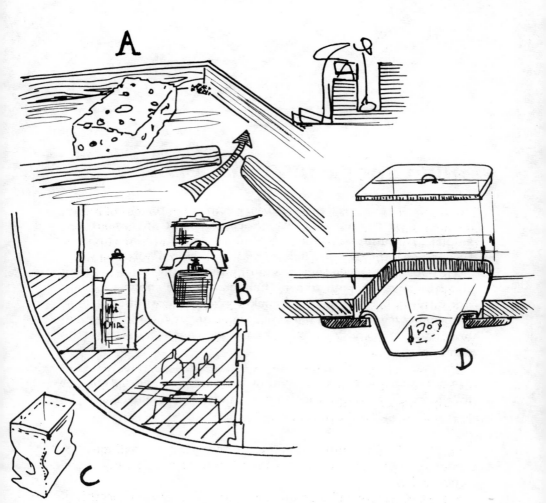

Sauces, Spices and Herbs

Cooking gets more and more exotic. Even on board, spiced dishes are becoming popular, so that various herbs and sauces garnish salads, grills and even hashes. Manufacturers nowadays produce these in elegant fashion, using small well closed bottles.

Why not make sure they are to hand when needed by having them in a rack for all to see, thus leaving the shelves for less attractive items? A small herb rack won't disfigure a sliding door, and won't weigh it down too much, especially if you add a vertical bracket at each end to help stiffen it and to act as handles on the door.

Powdered products like instant coffee, tea, sugar etc. will stay dry in jam jars. Hang them by their lids, screwed under a shelf or to a board fixed to the coachroof or under the side deck.

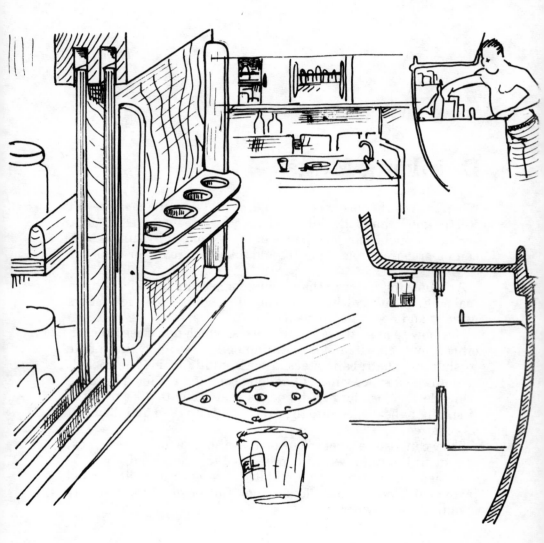

Drinking Mugs

When the weather is rough and cold, so that even the cook doesn't feel too good, that's the end of well prepared meals served at table.

For those who can, hot drinks or thick soups, anything which can be prepared from a packet and a kettle, are the order of the day.

And nothing is better than a mug for serving them in — but a real mug, cylindrical, heavy and of china, which holds heat, stays upright and doesn't spill easily.

But how to stow these bulky objects, which don't nest in each other? I put mine in a plastic drainpipe, split to allow the handle to slide in. The tube is stacked horizontally inside the cockpit coaming — a space which I had long sought a use for. The thing which looks like a large fish hook is snapped onto the rim of the first mug to be loaded into the tube, and I can then pull them out as required.

They can also be stacked one on the other in a tall plywood box, shown on the right, which can be fixed to a bulkhead.

A friend of mine made a gimballed stowage, rather like an old fashioned cradle, where four mugs, full or empty, sit snugly awaiting their owners.

Cooking under Sail

In anything but calm weather, the angle of heel of a sailing boat, added to the pitching motion brought on by choppy seas, can make life complicated down below.,

Wide open spaces which are nice and easy to clean, turn into bob-runs for anything placed at one end, and waves met at an awkward angle can take a delight in upsetting the pot so carefully set on the stove, even when gimballed.

Detachable fiddles, of reasonable height, will break up these open expanses if carefully sited, thus limiting the downhill movement of the miniature toboggans.

If these fiddles are going to be used often, it's a good idea to let small stainless steel, copper or bronze tubes into the worktops, at places where pegs in the fiddles can be slotted in to hold them in place. An old toothbrush will serve to clean these small holes from time to time.

Metal springs will hold pots on the stove. The one shown is easy enough to make from scrap alloy and a tensioning spring; one is needed on each side.

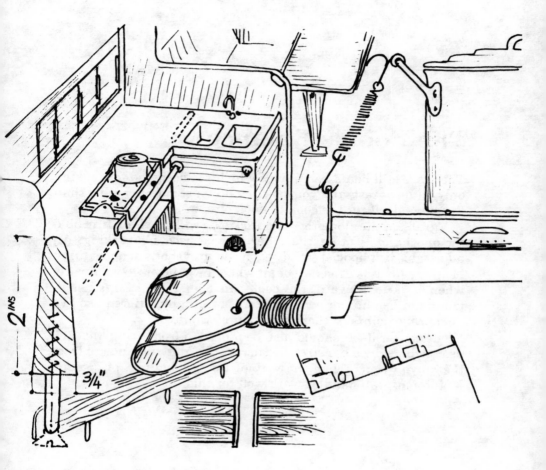

The Cook's Balance

There are still boats being built which are designed for cooking only while at rest, and you look in vain for something other than the stove itself for the cook to hook onto in a seaway.

A grab handle along the coachroof side will provide a firm hold for one hand, so that the other can be used for cooking. An adjustable belt hooked solidly each end to eyebolts at about thigh height, will be as good as a chair when the galley is to windward; when it is to leeward, the cook can lean forward against it. Optimum heights for each tack are marginally different, so two anchorage points at each end are preferable.

The cooker itself should also be protected from being knocked as it swings, by a bar stretched across the front (far enough from the stove not to get in the way of free gimballing, of course). Motorboat grab handles work well for this.

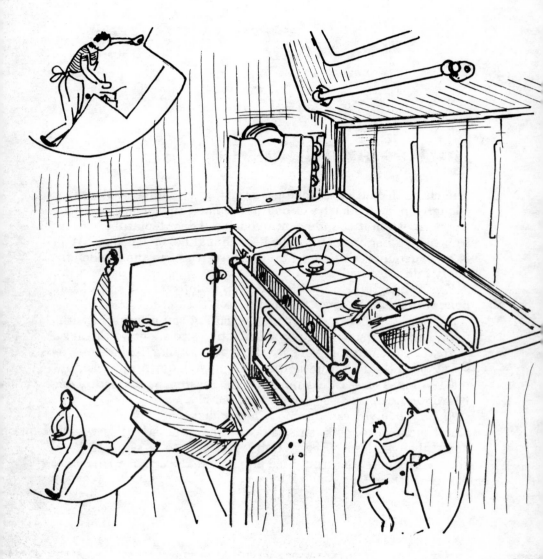

Bottles and Liquids

The chink of bottles knocking against one another is pleasant enough on a drinks tray, but it becomes tiresome and even worrying when it sounds continuously all day. Isolating bottles from each other has not always been thought of or, if designed in, is not adequate. Cruising families have risen to the challenge nobly and effectively.

Fig. A. Dinghy fittings include snap clamps for the spinnaker pole, which can be ideal for holding the neck of a bottle.

Fig. B. A thin strip of corrugated roofing can be covered with foam backed tape, to give a most effective and silent bottle rack.

Fig. C. Bars often dispense — what am I saying, they ration — spirits and the like from bottles held upside down in racks, by means of measures called optics; this is a system which is ideal on board (you can always pour two measures).

Fig. D. I have seen oil and vinegar dispensed by pipettes or small suction droppers. This enables flimsy plastic bottles, which don't always close properly and get sticky, to be emptied into stout containers like fruit juice jars, where the dropper can stay permanently.

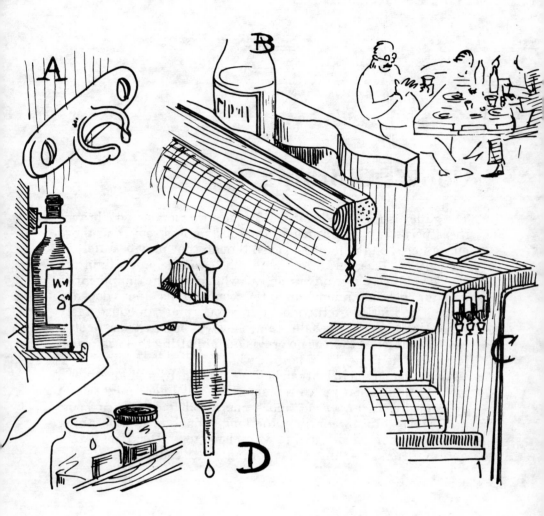

Cook's Clothing

The galley is full of risks at sea. To the crew member who braves these perils in a lumpy chop, they are no less real than those encountered on the foredeck, even though they may be different.

Properly placed grab rails and a belt can help maintain the cook's balance, as we have seen; but what about the equipment he uses for cooking and on which the results of his efforts depend? Knives and forks are the most dangerous, and can cause nasty wounds to anyone overbalancing; they will be sure to cut or stab sooner or later, if there is no provision for putting them safely on one side when they have been used.

Anything put on to boil can boil over, so that a knight's armour, an astronaut's suit or a fireman's protective gear might seem appropriate. In any case, shoes must be left on — sea boots preferably — and wear an apron long enough to stop anything hot being poured down into your boot tops. Don't just wear bathing trunks — think what boiling water could do . . .

Summary

And so we may now summarise those lessons learned as a result of putting to sea in many different galleys.

1. A high grab rail will allow the cook to hold on or stay steady.

2. A solid bar in front of the stove will protect it from the weight of the cook.

3. A belt will act as a seat, or something to lean forward against, thus leaving both hands free.

4. The space under the stove should be waterproof.

5. A safe spot for knives in use must be provided.

6. Fiddles and dividers should be at least two inches high.

7. All drawers should latch automatically in the closed position.

8. All deep shelves and drawers should have dividers to stop contents moving about in the rolling plane.

9. Drawers tailored to fit the side of the boat give a little extra room.

10. Small items can be picked out in deep lockers more easily if the shelves are divided, so that some of the contents are on the back of the door.

11. Any locker which is very difficult to get at should be reserved for those items which are only seldom wanted.

12. There should be some means of wedging cooking pots on the stove, not only to hold them steady, but to keep them balanced even if the stove isn't gimballed.

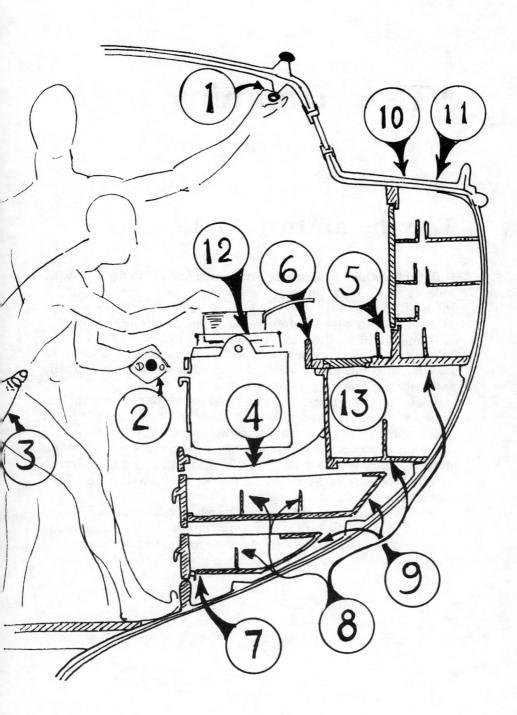

VII   Dinghies

Towing an Inflatable

Inflatables which have neither transom nor rigid floor, seem to be able to get up incredible speed when they are drifting by themselves, blown by the wind (have you ever tried swimming after one?), but also to offer considerable resistance to forward movement when being rowed.

When towing, this resistance will be reduced quite a lot if the bow is lifted out of the water, but there is the danger that the inflatable will capsize as soon as the wind freshens.

Try using three lines. Make one fast each side to the hand line which runs round the whole boat; these are then tied to the aft pulpit to make sure that the dinghy steers properly. The third line is the painter running from a strongpoint on the bow (or through a ring on the bow to a strongpoint further aft); this is tied high up on the backstay to hoist the inflatable's bow well clear of the water. The system works well.

Finally, a better waterflow can be assured, if separation from the underside of the hull is encouraged by sticking a foam wedge between the skin of the aft air chamber and a strip of neoprene, in the form of a permanent trim tab right across the stern.

Rigid Dinghies

Some rigid dinghies yaw wildly from side to side of the wake. The Optimist class is one of these, but it sometimes has to assume the role of ship's tender for the sake of the younger members of the family, who want to sail it on reaching harbour.

Two small skegs in hardwood will cure the problem, and will also help to protect the bottom when the boat is hauled over gravel or a concrete slipway.

The drawing is fairly explicit. I fitted them without backing pieces and the skegs didn't move so, though these are shown and it is better to fit them, they aren't essential if care is used.

For short trips, if the dinghy is not too heavy, it can be hoisted by the topping lift or a whip rigged to the backstay. The hoist should be rigged to a bridle running on the centreline of the dinghy between its main thwart and the transom, and two steadying lines are fitted fore and aft to makeshift davits over the aft pulpit. The dinghy is then hauled up until its gunwale is resting on the mother ship's transom.

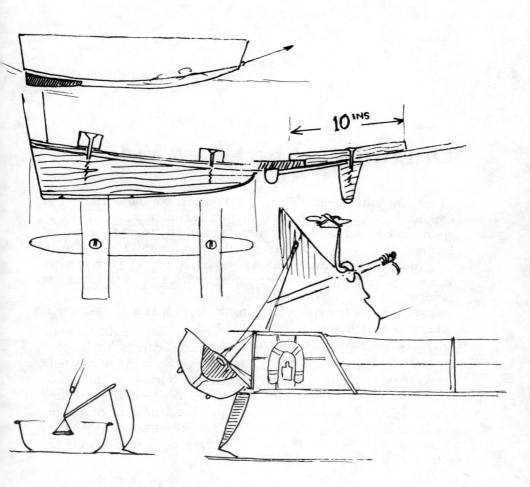

Dinghies at the Quay Wall

There are still harbours without floating pontoons. If it is a popular resort, there is a risk that round about noon and again at six o'clock, dinghies will proliferate at the bottom of the ladder leading up to the quay nearest to the best (or only) bar in town.

If your mooring line isn't long enough, those who arrive after you won't be able to move your dinghy back so as to reach the ladder themselves. Think of others.

Also you run the risk of having to cross a raft of dinghies if others haven't had your forethought.

You can always moor your dinghy a little way off and pull it in by a whip.

Wheels

I spend quite a large part of my holidays at one spot, near my step-mother who lives on one side of the harbour, while my quayside berth is on the other. Rather than walk 300 or 400 yards several times a day, I prefer to use an old dinghy to scull thirty yards or so.

But the concrete slipway is very rough for the 5–6 yard pull each trip. Even with metal straps, the two skegs wouldn't last a season.

I made up the little gadget shown opposite: two nylon wheels run on braced axles bolted to stainless steel cheek plates, which are screwed to the after ends of the skegs. They are, of course, only any good on concrete, but they work very well and don't make the slightest difference to the boat in the water, even under tow.

Rowing an Inflatable

Rowing an inflatable against a short chop whipped up by a fresh breeze is a somewhat uncertain affair. This is because of its short, relatively heavy oars with small blades, working in rowlocks which are too near the surface of the water.

I once had occasion to take out a mooring line in a rather exposed anchorage in order to give the boat better holding power. I took a single paddle, just to see whether the pulling power of one man canoe fashion (which I had done seriously in my time) was enough in an inflatable.

It is without doubt the best system, and it is a skill quickly learned (repeated figures of eight).

It is slightly more tiring in a flat calm without any wind, because the arms have to do all the steering (a breeze will hold the boat's head off one way, while you can paddle on one side against it). But, if you can't have proper oars with proper blades, have one or even two paddles available.

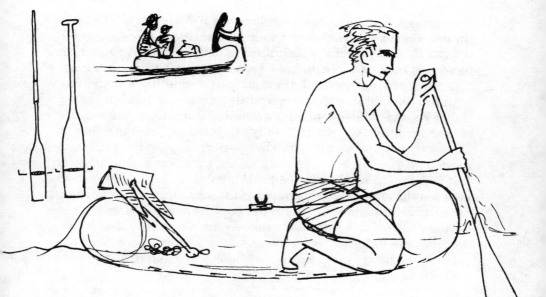

Inflate, Deflate

Having to get all that air either into or out of an inflatable is one of the drawbacks of an amenity which, nevertheless, has some good points. The ten minutes which it takes to blow it up by foot or by hand (not more, see the maker's brochure), can seem a very long time on a baking hot, still day. But that's small beer compared with the time it takes to get every last drop of air out of the brute before stowing it away for a long passage; only on big boats can a rubber dinghy be carried fully inflated — whether it is athwartships or fore and aft, there's normally just not enough room.

It can sometimes be carried partly deflated and folded in two between the mast and the inner forestay. One discovery has been to use a car vacuum cleaner, running off the ship's battery. It can do the bulk of the inflation and, above all, it makes a lot of difference to deflation when reversed.

If the bellows are broken, a diaphragm bilge pump can sometimes make shift instead.

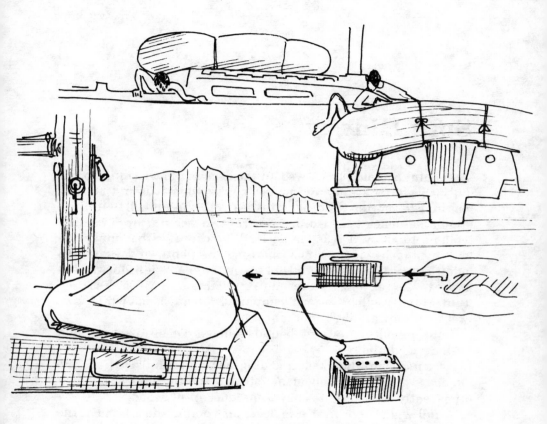

Split Dinghy

A big dinghy could be stowed on the deck of quite a small boat if only the latter's mast didn't get in the way. It is not usually possible to shorten the dinghy to the point where it will fit into the available space because, if you want to keep a large enough volume to carry a reasonable load, you must either make the dinghy much wider or else increase the depth of the hull. In addition, you have to maintain plenty of beam right forward in order to keep as long a waterline as possible, or it will sink so deep that stability will be seriously impaired. Result: a boat which is as wet as an inflatable, if not more so.

But ingenuity knows no bounds when it comes to achieving a well defined aim!

An American who liked rigid dinghies, and wanted to have one on board his small day-boat, adopted the solution opposite, which apparently proved quite easy to produce in plywood.

A full width floor timber is necessary across the aft end of the gap, in order to spread the load of the passengers. A bit of work with ¼ in marine ply will do the rest, screwed and glued to brackets or knees.

All items should be carefully offered up cold, even screwed in position, and then adjusted, before being dismantled and reassembled this time with glue. The insertion piece can be used for storage.

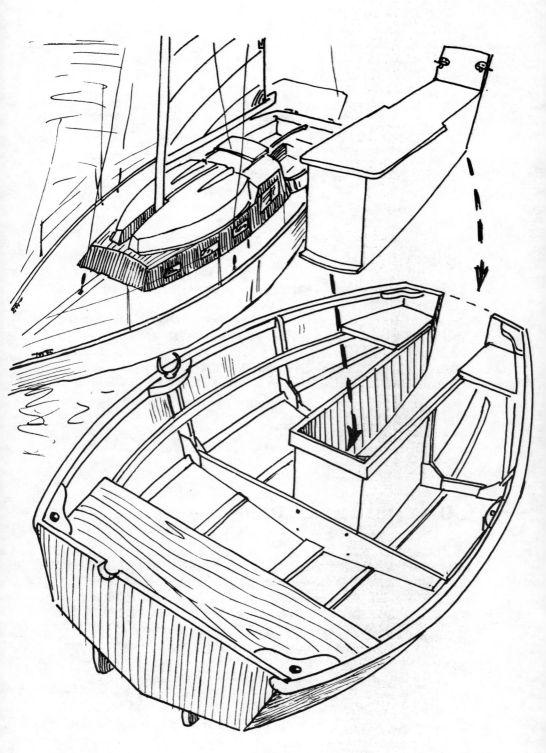

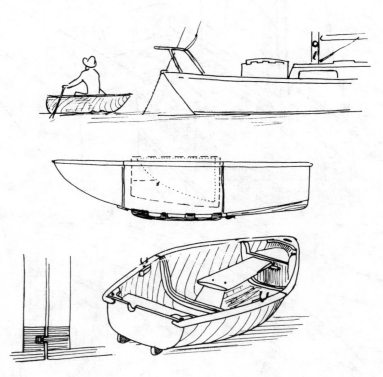

Collapsible Dinghy

As the reader may have noticed in this section, I don't like inflatables very much. Of all the good explanations which I can offer, only one defies close examination — or rather two.

My two nephews accompany me sometimes. Self-effacing on passage, they open up on reaching port and, in exchange for operating a shuttle service to and from the landing stage, they have the right to the remaining use of the dinghy for exploring, racing or general amusement.

I therefore need a boat which will both stand up to the broken bottles, tin cans and other detritus which strews the foreshore where we sometimes stop, and which will also sail — not only for my nephews' sakes, but also sometimes for my own amusement.

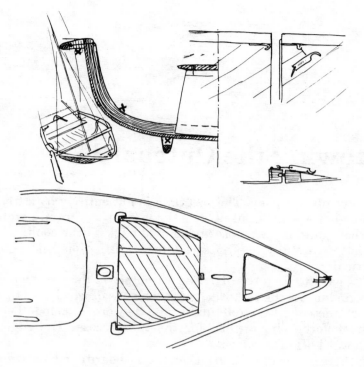

I drew this little fellow specifically to fit my own boat. Dismantled, the fore part stows in the stern, which in turn nests in the middle section; it all fits happily between the mast and the inner forestay. Eight inches of deck is left each side for passage, and the grab handles which serve as bilge keels for the dinghy make this a reasonable amount.

Perfectionist, I made it in moulded ply to save weight. It is, in fact very light, but at what a cost! (in time and labour, I mean).

The joints are watertight. One frame, made of laminated wood, has a tongue which fits into a neoprene foam-filled groove in its partner on the next section.

Stainless steel snap locks ensure a close fit, and assembly takes five minutes. An inflatable would only begin to look like a boat in this time. The rowing thwart (which doubles as a dagger board when sailing), oars and spars all stack under the mattress of one of the quarter berths on board.

185

Stowing the Outboard

It's not always easy. The fuel tank is not entirely leak free, the motor spits a little oil, it gets dirty from use in oily water in harbour, and it always seems to hold back a little cooling water which it carefully regurgitates later . . . It is thus better stowed vertically.

It's easy to fix a board on the aft pulpit, at the point where an upstand meets the rail. Each of two blocks of wood is as thick as the diameter of the pulpit tubing, and they are fitted together with bolts before being drilled for the tube recess. The edges are smoothed off afterwards.

If there is a deep enough locker, the outboard can also be stowed vertically inside it, secure from the attentions of thieves. However, it would be wise to close off any engine stowage from the rest of the locker's contents.

Fitting out a Dinghy for Youngsters

There's not much to turning an inflatable into a fine yacht for a youngster — providing there aren't too many Optimists or Penguins about to show it up.

A keel isn't difficult; a single leeboard is all that is needed, at one side. It should be mounted on a beam whose end is reinforced to four thicknesses, so that it can accept the bolt which will serve as a pivot. The drawing on the left shows the method, using a 2 inch bolt of ½ inch diameter. This gives enough support for a small board the size of a tennis racket. Made of ½ in plywood, it is about 2 ft 6 in x 1 ft.

The cross beam should be strapped to another placed in the bottom of the boat before it is inflated, so that all is held in place. This makes the mast easy to solve (fit a step on the lower cross beam). The rudder is also easy, even though it has a pivoting blade. It is mounted on an outboard bracket — which is worth getting specially, if you don't want to become involved in tricky glueing processes.

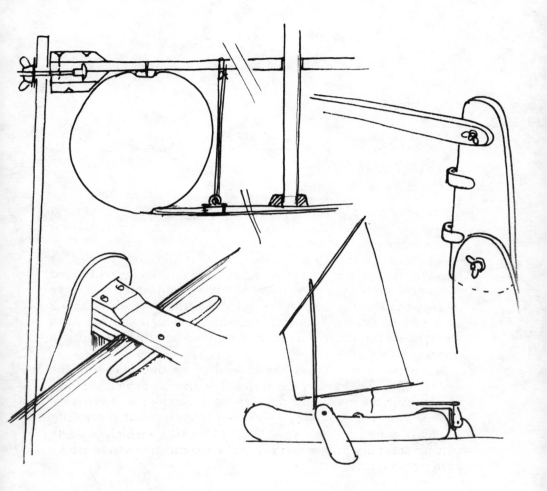